PRECIOUS WHISPERS

PRECIOUS WHISPERS

The Aftermath

Marie-Rose Fox

CHALLENGER II PTY LTD

First Printing, 2022

ISBN: Paperback 978-0-6485913-3-7
        EPub 978-0-6485913-4-4

Besides my dear husband Stephen, I can think of only one person to whom I am honoured to dedicate this book, my wonderful friend and mentor Heather. I have known this kind, charismatic lady since shortly after my family emigrated to Australia in 1971, and I feel extremely blessed to have her in my life. Words are merely a channel through which we can transmit our thoughts and feelings, thus I am making use of this opportunity to transport my message of gratitude to a wonderful human being who took me under her wing when it mattered the most.

So, Heather, this is for you, my friend. Enjoy reading about events you're already familiar with, although you may be seeing a different version than your own perspective as you read the contents through my eyes. Thank you for sharing your life with me and allowing mine to be a part of yours.

CONTENTS

CONTENTS

Introduction

A Word From Marie-Rose

Just a little background for any readers who haven't read my first book title *Hidden Thorns*, written in memory of my beautiful only child Michelle, who was brutally murdered by her then partner Adam on the Gold Coast, Australia, in November 2007. I was born in Portugal, grew up in France, and have lived in Australia since my late teens. Writing my life story was by far the most difficult project I've ever had to undertake. This included above all the cruel loss of my daughter at such a young age, the murder investigation and court case that followed, dealing with grief and pain, my battle with cancer in 2014, and so much more.

But against all odds and with divine intervention, *Hidden Thorns* was completed and subsequently published in November 2018. I'm extremely grateful for that. Nothing substantial and meaningful in life is ever easy. But if by persevering to the end in writing my story, people's hearts have been touched, my purpose is accomplished, and I couldn't be happier. I can almost hear God whispering tenderly in my ear the words from Scripture: "You have done well, good and faithful servant!" (Matthew 25:21, NIRV).

Since its release, *Hidden Thorns* has been making an impact on people's lives far beyond my wildest expectations. On one occasion, a lady contacted me for a copy. With deep sadness, she shared that her son had committed suicide and *Hidden Thorns* had been recommended as a book that could help her find peace amidst her devastating grief. Many others have contacted me or posted reviews, sharing how they read my story, then passed it on to family members and friends who have experienced the loss of a loved one to help them deal with their heartbreak.

That so many individuals took the time to acknowledge that my story had touched their hearts and made a powerful impact on their lives has left me almost speechless. In 2019, *Hidden Thorns* was one of three finalists at the Australasian CALEB (Christian Authors Lifting Each Other's Books) awards, which recognise the best in Australasian Christian writing. I was so grateful to God because I'd given my all in writing this story. The responses from my readers was my reward even more than being a finalist. Then again, I shouldn't have been surprised because God was responsible for making this a reality, not me. So to all of you out there who invested in purchasing my book, may I express a sincere thank you.

All that said, the whole experience of writing my ever-so-emotional first book left me spiritually spent and exhausted. When death steals a child from this world, it also robs the surviving parents of an expressed identity. A wife without her husband is called a widow. A husband without his wife is a widower. A child bereft of parents is referred to as an orphan. But there is no specific word in the English language to describe a parent who has lost a child. It's just an undefined hollow of hurt that no one but God understands. Pushing my way through that hurt to write my first book was too painful to even consider repeating the process.

I recall being asked the almost unavoidable question at an author's interview with Omega Writers, an organisation that educates, supports, and inspires Australasian Christian writers towards excellence across a range of genres. My answer was simply that I had no plans to write anything else in the near future. But it's obvious to me now that God had a bigger plan for me that I was unaware of at that particular time. I came to realise that the incredible journey on which God has taken me is still ongoing and filled with many more experiences He is calling me to share, including many lessons of healing and spiritual development God has taught me during the aftermath of loss and grief.

That, dear reader, is how this sequel *Precious Whispers* came about. Why this title? The Bible tells us that with faith as small as a mustard seed, nothing is impossible (Matthew 17:20), and if planted in good soil, this tiny mustard seed will grow into a full tree (Mark 4:30-32; Luke 13:18-19). That good soil is a heart open to hear from God (Matthew 13:18-23).

Similarly, when God speaks to me, His precious whisper in my ear usually starts with a tiny idea He lays on my heart that grows as I am obedient to His voice into a full-blown fruitful harvest. I shared in *Hidden Thorns* how more than seven years after my daughter's murder, I underwent surgery for tongue cancer. As I lay recovering in bed at home, unable to speak due to the excruciating pain, I heard God's sweet voice.

I'd experienced visions before this, including one that told me where my daughter had been buried. But this time when I couldn't even speak aloud, God's precious whispering voice spoke audibly to my mind and heart, promising full healing and calling me to share my story with others. My obedience to God's voice then led to writing *Hidden Thorns*. My obedience to God's voice now has led to writing this sequel, *Precious Whispers*. Not just to share my ongoing journey but more importantly for God's glory.

Throughout writing *Precious Whispers*, I have learned to depend on God and pray about everything. That in itself is a real test of my faith because God has a habit of testing those He loves. These valuable lessons that have emerged from His precious whispers have definitely made me stronger and kept me on the right path, guiding me through my everyday life as I am willing to stop and listen to God's still, small voice.

As you read the following pages, it is my hope and prayer that you will catch a glimpse of how greatly and lovingly God has helped my husband Stephen and I go through the highs and lows of our lives, both emotionally and spiritually. And that in so doing, you will glimpse how greatly God loves you as well. Only God's grace has made it possible for me to move forward in life as the loss of my only child in such an unjust, cruel way is a sorrow that will never completely dissipate. Since I am far from a perfect person, I look up to God to help me get through my darkest days.

My other immediate wish for you, dear reader, is that you'll find an abundance of meaningful and inspirational material within these pages to meditate on. Meditation doesn't mean putting your mind in neutral and thinking about nothing. It means pondering about what you are reading, thus enabling you to adapt it to your own circumstances. I hope and pray that you will find much in the following chapters to help you in whatever circumstances you are going through and to bless you both spiritually and emotionally.

Or perhaps you have someone in your sphere of family and friends you know would benefit greatly from this read because of what they are going through. So why not be a blessing and share it with them. Let me also add here that if you haven't yet read *Hidden Thorns*, may I recommend doing so just because many stories in *Precious Whispers* take place in the context of previous events told in *Hidden Thorns*.

My heartfelt thanks to each of you, dear readers, for picking up this book and joining me on the rest of my journey because ...

Time is too slow for those who wait,
too swift for those who fear,
too long for those who grieve,
too short for those who rejoice.
But for those who love, time is eternity.
~ Henry Van Dyke (1852-1933)

2 |

My Girl

The festivity of Jesus's birth has been so meaningful to me for as long as I could remember. From childhood, it was all about being together with family and all that represented. The contagious laughter around the table as we shared succulent food and beverages. Eggnog. Christmas pudding. Or my own favourite, the *bûche de Noël*, or Yule log, a jelly-roll style chocolate cake filled with chocolate cream that is a traditional French Christmas dessert.

In the dazzling red and green atmosphere of Christmas tree and decorations, the anticipation of what awaited us under the tree was almost unbearable. The temptation to rush over and open the gifts or peek into the stockings to discover what Santa had put there grew by the minute. So much so, in fact, that it took an unbelievable amount of self-control to wait like everyone else. But while all the above portrays family love, the true "reason for the season" which made our homes at Christmas a centre of joy is the celebration of God's ultimate gift, the birth of Jesus, the Christ Child. That's the real feeling of Christmas. Waking up on that special morning with a grin from ear to ear and a heart full of hope because God is in our midst, showing His great love for us. Christmas can be a time to heal and renew our strength. A time to enjoy the season and to rejoice as well.

Christmas became even more special to me after the birth of my only daughter Michelle in early December 1978, my precious Christmas gift from God. It was Michelle's favourite season of the year too as we celebrated both her birth and the Christ Child's.

But in December 2007, our first Christmas without Michelle, that feeling was no longer there. Everything that had made the Christmas season a time of rejoicing in the past had now become mourning. First had come the grief of her sudden disappearance on November 27, 2007. Then just a few days later came her long-term boyfriend Adam's confession of her murder, which subsequently led police on December 5, 2007, to where he had buried her body. My picture-perfect Christmas and the heart-busting joy it represented had been stolen from me without warning.

On Christmas Day just three weeks later, I didn't know what to do with myself. How on earth was I supposed to live with this impossible grief? I sought refuge in my study. There I began jotting down words that came to mind with an inexplicable urgency, desperately trying to express what my broken heart was telling me. Addressing Michelle through a poem was difficult but seemed right because it made me feel she was still close by me in some supernatural way.

I finished the poem. Then I tucked it away "somewhere safe" like so many other treasures and memories of Michelle I didn't want to lose but would rather not revisit because the mere thought of them hurt too much. The trouble with parking something "somewhere safe" is that in time it gets overlooked or misplaced or even voluntarily forgotten. That's okay too.

After the loss of Michelle, my husband Stephen and I relocated to Warwick, Queensland, about two and a half hours' drive inland from our previous home on the Gold Coast and too distant from my extended family in Sydney to easily visit for Christmas. As the years passed, the Christmas season remained a difficult time of heartbreaking memories. I'd long lost track of that poem I'd written.

Then a decade after losing Michelle, the most unusual occurrence took place. Those tenderly expressed emotions and thoughts written long ago popped up right out of the blue in one of Stephen's email files. Fancy that! Stephen thought at the time, and rightly so, that it was rather odd for my words to appear on his computer when they should have logically been stashed away on mine.

Of course, it didn't take me long to realise why. That roughly put together poem I'd written out of intense grief on a piece of paper was so precious to me that I'd typed it into my computer. I'd saved it in a personal memorabilia file I'd dedicated to "My Girl," which enabled me to indulge those "oh so special" random moments when nostalgia overwhelmed me beyond comprehension. Namely, those dreaded anniversary dates so hard to dismiss like birthdays and holidays. I'd also automatically sent my husband a copy for safekeeping.

After rereading what had been written out of a mother's grieving heart on that first Christmas without her child, I decided to update the poem in case I found the courage and strength to read it to her on that special time of year she was so fond of during her much too short life. Allow me to share it with you. The words still move me to tears.

My Girl
I'm sad that you left me without saying goodbye,
For life without you gets harder as time goes by.
I can't help but wonder how things could have been.
You see, suddenly you were nowhere to be seen!
Now then, whose favourite time of year is here again?
Yours! It's not much fun without you, my best friend.
My heart hurts as it's clear you didn't plan to leave early.
As for me, I'll always regret not having said, "I'm sorry."
Time to say goodbye and Merry Christmas, my darling.
Time to celebrate Jesus's birth with God, King of kings.
Truth is, it's impossible for us to see or hug one another.
But know that you'll be remembered in my heart forever.
Love you always,
Mum

PS: By the way, Michelle, since writing the above poem,
I've written my memoir, your legacy.
I will need your Twitter account to send you a copy.
The book's title is Hidden Thorns: A True Story.
It's doing very well. I think you'd be proud of me.

Finding that poem from long ago was a blessing beautifully orchestrated by God. Indeed, painful feelings that have been hidden in the deep recesses of our hearts often manifest themselves through our tears. It is one way we deal with our emotions. In bringing this poem to light, God was simply reminding me that while losing my daughter still hurts, I have His assurance that one day my sweet girl and I will be reunited forever in Paradise.

That is your loving heavenly Father's promise to you as well if you have placed your trust in Him.

3

Surviving The Aftermath

The aftermath is something that results or follows from an event. The word is often used in context of circumstances so disastrous and unbearable that surviving them and going on with any type of normal life in the aftermath becomes very difficult. This so aptly describes what became of my life after my daughter's murder.

For a while after losing Michelle, I was still dreaming about what could have been, imagining a different kind of future, the future I would normally have expected to unfold with my daughter as time passed. When I lost sight of that dream, everything crumbled so that my heart broke in a million pieces when it should have been going through its mending process. Sometimes these circumstances felt so surreal I feared they could easily send me back to that dark pit where life felt without any hope, purpose, or anything resembling a future. Long ago, I'd vowed never to allow myself to feel that hopeless again.

Focussing On the Positive Versus the Negative

It is for this reason, dear reader, that I refuse to give life to any negative thought trying to creep in whenever I let my guard down with the intent of dangerously messing with my mind. The Bible talks about how we can be taken captive by wrong, negative thoughts if we don't intentionally take our thoughts captive in obedience to Christ.

> *Take captive every thought to make it obedient to Christ. (2 Corinthians 10:5)*
>
> *See to it that no one takes you captive through hollow and deceptive philosophy . . . rather than on Christ . . . Set your hearts on things above, where Christ is, seated at the right hand of God. (Colossians 2:8; 3:1)*
>
> *Whatever is true, whatever is noble, whatever is right, whatever is pure, whatever is lovely, whatever is admirable—if anything is excellent or praiseworthy—think about such things. And the God of peace will be with you. (Philippians 4:8)*

In other words, when those negative, dark thoughts threaten to overwhelm me, I know that I must take captive those thoughts before they can take me captive. I need to rebuke the negative thoughts as they come and instead focus my thoughts on Christ and on the positive things Christ brings into my life.

Negativity is a serious feeling not to be ignored because it is most effective when vulnerability is present, giving it the power to become depression disguised as the easy way out. Being vulnerable happens when we allow our anxious thoughts to branch off in all directions instead of focussing them on Christ. That's when we need to voice our trust in God loud and clear so we can keep focussed on God's grace in the present moment instead of the painful memories of past events.

I know this because I've been there. If it weren't for my faith and God's grace, I would still be there or not be here at all. I was very lucky to have survived that horrible phase in my life. No, wait! Let me rephrase that. I was truly blessed to have survived! So today when God wants to get my attention, I stop, listen, and obey no matter what. After all, my future is in God's hands, and He knows what's best for me. He promises that everything happening to us, no matter how painful, is ultimately for our good if we love God and are fitting into His plans.

> *And we know that in all things God works for the good of those who love him, who have been called according to his purpose. (Romans 8:28)*

Learning to Look Forward

In the meantime, I shall continue walking with my heavenly Father, looking forward to those blessings He has for me, and enjoying each moment because I know I can trust Him implicitly. This new normal I find myself in, the continued aftermath of losing my only child, has definitely ushered me into a life that is quite foreign to the one I knew before the unthinkable disrupted my world. That was the day my music died, leaving me no real reason to sing or dance anymore because my heart was broken and I didn't know how to repair it.

But I've gradually come to realise that this is my new reality, and as difficult as it may be, I'm slowly coming to terms with it. Allow me to put it another way. Imagine life as an orchestra constantly playing beautiful symphonies where every artistic work or opus has its own unique structure scored specifically for *your* orchestra. As far as I was concerned, my own personal symphony was outstanding because it was perfectly written for me. Then the Phantom of the Opera snuck in from behind like a thief in the night and stole that perfectly scored opus so that the orchestra is now playing random notes without any rhythm or structure.

All that music analogy may be more than you feel is needed rather than just going straight to the point. But using vivid imagery and story often helps a message become easier to understand, so I hope you will be patient with me in sharing these with you. In fact, this is an art of expressing one's thoughts Jesus used frequently in the Bible. When He compares the kingdom of God to a mustard seed or yeast (Matthew 13:31-33) or God's Word to a farmer sowing seed (Matthew 13:1-9) or calls Himself the Bread of Life or Light of the World (John 6:35; 8:12) or compares His followers to salt, light, or a city on a hill (Matthew 5:13-16), He is using visual imagery and analogy to make a point.

So if it worked for Jesus, I figure my analogy of an orchestra will work for me. And in truth, it's okay to admit finding ourselves in a weird state of mind occasionally even if that means letting others know our life is like an out-of-tune orchestra that has lost its music score. It simply means we're not afraid to expose our vulnerabilities to others. We are not ashamed of who we are and what took us to that place. Despite the present cacophony of our life music, we have faith we will overcome the situation we're in because our loving heavenly Father is present with us at every step guiding us along the right path. All we have to do now is to master the act of listening to God's precious whispers so we can learn to move forward in His steps.

That said, this isn't an easy task to master. Just a few steps away from the true path on which God has called us to walk are dark pits of self-pity and despair or side trails of pride and self-will. If we don't learn to look forward, keeping our eyes focussed on the path to which God has called us, we can soon find ourselves stepping over the edge into a deep pit or getting lost on a trail that leads into a dangerous wilderness. Even well-meaning friends can lead us astray if we let them usurp God's place in our lives.

The reality is that many individuals are set on following the easiest or most popular path because they see everyone else taking that path. A road that looks less travelled seems unappealing. We may wonder why no one else is travelling that way. When we arrive at a major turning point in our journey such as a fork in the road, it becomes a very important decision time. Are we going to allow peer pressure or the opinions of friends and family help us choose which path to take? Or are we going to keep our eyes looking forward and focussed on the true path God has called us to follow? We can either take directions from the light of His smile or the cloud of His refusal.

So how do we know which way to go? Simply put, God's Word is our road map for the Christian way of life God wants us to follow.

In fact, you could say that BIBLE stands for **B**asic **I**nstructions **B**efore **L**eaving **E**arth. God will always show us in His Word which way to go. But like any parent, He would prefer to be asked first.

When our circumstances don't make sense to us, aren't fair, or we think we don't deserve what we've been dished out in the moment, that is when we need to take matters to God in prayer. Once we've prayed about it, that's when we get what I call a spiritual "second wind," much like a leap of faith to keep following God's directions, trusting it's the right path for us. As we learn to look forward, we can make our life's choices, whatever they may be, with confidence, knowing that God always has our back as King David tells us in the thirty-seventh psalm.

> *The Lord makes firm the steps of the one who delights in him; though he may stumble, he will not fall, for the Lord upholds him with his hand. (Psalm 37:23-24)*

Yes, we may stumble from time to time along the path. But so long as we keep our focus obediently on God and delight ourselves in Him, then even in the dark aftermath of life's catastrophes, we won't need to worry about falling into those steep pits or getting lost on a side trail because our heavenly Father is holding us tightly by His own mighty, loving hand every step of the way.

4

Stand Up And Be Heard

Renowned American country singer Dolly Parton once commented: "A peacock that sits on its feathers is just another goose." If you aren't acquainted with these colourful creatures, peacocks boast impressively sized patterned plumage they fan out for display purposes such as seeking to attract a mate. There is a lot of truth in this quote. In fact, we see the same truth in the popular song by Aussie singer John Farnham "You're The Voice." Its bold statement to "stand together" and raise our voices to make it clear we refuse to live in fear and silence speaks volumes about choosing to "display our plumage" and make a difference in our world.

Yet I sense many of us sing along to the lyrics because we like the song and respect the singer rather than grasping its true meaning, which from my perspective is to stand up for a cause we feel strongly about.

The immediate cause that comes to my mind being the one staring us in the face right now—domestic violence. One purpose in writing *Hidden Thorns* was to raise awareness of such violence in hopes of encouraging women especially not to take chances they may later regret. I've been very troubled to see the rates of domestic violence continue rising so dramatically in our society.

So without further ado, I am putting my hand up and taking on the challenge not to be a goose any longer but to build up the courage to spread open my feathers like a true peacock does with such panache. I believe in the importance of this particular issue, and I will do everything in my power to bring attention to this crisis and make a substantial difference in ending domestic violence.

On that note, I'm inviting you, my reader, to join me in working together to destroy this cancer that is sickening our society to the core. The truth is that not everyone will share the same opinion on how to handle the issue, and there will always be obstacles when it comes to voicing our opinion in public. But we mustn't lose heart or be afraid to speak up instead of being bystanders because we are facing a sad reality that must be addressed without delay.

Not convinced yet this is a real problem? Please humour me and turn on your television set. Or hop onto your favourite social media platform. It's there screaming out for help wherever you look. You may say,   "Okay, I see what you mean. But shouldn't we let the authorities deal with this? Isn't that enough?"

To which I would reply, "A fair comment. It certainly should be enough. But guess what! If it was enough to just leave it to the authorities, it wouldn't keep on happening."

You might also suggest, "Hey, you're biased on this topic because you're a direct victim of domestic violence. I understand why you're so passionate about voicing your opinion because you've experienced personally the repercussions of what domestic violence can do to a person or a family. But your experience doesn't mean we all need to support this particular cause."

"You're absolutely right I am biased!" I would respond. There is no doubt that what happened to me was devastating. But even if circumstances were different, I would have supported this cause.

Why? Because long before my Michelle was murdered, countless innocent lives were being taken in vain by their domestic partners, in part due to the lack of awareness and support from their peers or society in general. Sadly, many women are too frightened to report assaults to the authorities for fear of not being heard or believed—or even worse, of being mocked. So they continue putting up with violent acts from offenders day in and day out until they've had enough. Then the minute they stop fighting for their own safety, tragedy strikes.

Someone else might add, "This world is filled with evil acts no one can prevent. What makes your cause different?"

I would respond, "It's different because a majority of the crimes committed as a result of domestic violence could have been prevented. Which can mean only one thing. We need people in place ready to listen and act when it counts."

The Victoria Police Family Violence Command reports ninety-three thousand family violence incidents a year. It hasn't helped that there has been a historical culture of considering domestic violence a personal family matter so that police have been reluctant to intervene short of actual murder. To top it off, when police do put offenders behind bars, the law is often far too lenient. Offenders get away with a slap on the wrist, then keep on re-offending because they know they can get away with it. Let me share some specifics from my own state of Queensland as example.

The Hannah Clarke Story

Hannah Clarke was a young Australian mother whose life was cut horrifically short along with those of her three small children on February 19, 2020, in Camp Hill, Queensland, when her estranged husband

Rowan Baxter poured fuel into the interior of her car, then set it on fire. The husband then took his own life. The investigation that followed the murders revealed that Baxter had a history of domestic violence, including in public so that bystanders had called the police. Hannah Clarke had a protection order against Baxter at the time of the murders due to credible fears that he was increasingly dangerous.

Baxter had never been held accountable because none of his previous acts, including one count of child kidnapping and endangerment just weeks before the murders, rose to the level of criminal behaviour according to current domestic violence legislation. Because of this, the police refused to intervene. The shocking murders have sparked a national debate about Australia's epidemic of domestic violence, including calls for better counselling programs and training for police on issues of domestic violence. If such protections had been in place at the time, perhaps Hannah Clarke and her children might still be alive today.

Doreen Langham Murder

On February 22, 2021, Doreen Langham died in a horrific house fire south of Brisbane that was set by her former long-term boyfriend Gary Hely after he doused Doreen and her home with petrol. The case roused national outrage when it was learned that Doreen had called the police that very night to report Hely's presence outside her residence. After responding and speaking briefly to Doreen, the police made no further investigation nor offered any protection. Hely simply waited until the police left to break in and commit his heinous crime.

The perceived inaction from the police was compounded by the information that the police had been informed of threats by Hely on several occasions in preceding months. In fact, Hely had been served a domestic violence protective order to stay away from Doreen only ten days before the murder. During the inquiry, one Queensland police officer broke down in tears as she recalled meeting personally with a desperate and frightened Doreen just days before Doreen was killed. She acknowledged that with better training the police might have responded differently.

The state coroner also noted that the police officers involved had not acted with any intention of neglect or malice. The shortcomings in police response that led to Doreen Langham's death were judged as due to lack of training as well as acute understaffing in the police force.

When Protectors Are Offenders

Another problem arises when the very people who are supposed to protect Australians from domestic violence are the perpetrators. A 2020 ABC news report showcased a number of incidents where women experienced years of violence and abuse by spouses or life partners who were police officers. It also documented the reluctance of police to take action against other badged officers. The report called for an overhaul of policies for dealing with domestic violence reports involving serving officers, including identifying conflicts of interest so that police are not allowed to investigate close colleagues.

A Welcome Breakthrough

There have been several steps in the right direction as a result of some of these high-profile domestic violence killings. Legislation has been introduced to establish criminally enforceable federal family violence orders with breaches carrying a penalty of up to two years in prison.

A women's safety taskforce has also been set up by the Queensland government to examine and make improvements on how police officers investigate domestic and family violence. Among practical recommendations have been improved training for frontline officers to better recognise the signs of coercive control as well as how to respond to domestic violence calls.

A second recommendation has been a "One Stop Shop" at every police station where victims can report domestic violence, speak to an onsite social worker, and get immediate help as needed. This should include providing victims, primarily women and children, with a place of refuge where they can be sure they are safe, protected, and out of harm's way as well as services to counsel and empower them so they can pick themselves up and move on towards a brighter future.

In my own state of Queensland, the police commissioner has recently conceded that the initial responses and language used by officers investigating rape complaints are inappropriate and insensitive, including the perpetuating of outdated rape myths that choose to disbelieve the victim reporting rape. In consequence, the Gold Coast Centre Against Sexual Violence (GCCASV) will be pioneering among Queensland police departments a specialised sexual violence training program called "Start By Believing" to help police officers improve their initial response to rape and other sexual violence victims.

Not Enough

That said, police training is not on its own a "silver bullet" that will immediately reform police responses. Especially since many senior police officers and members of the influential police union have been strongly opposed to these inquiries and their recommendations. Nor are training programs an excuse for continuing to ignore the voices of women whose experiences have again and again demanded a true change within core police culture, not another "patchwork" fix designed not to ruffle too many feathers.

Sadly, recent cases like Hannah Clarke and Doreen Langham demonstrate that our police departments remain too slow in responding to desperate calls pouring in daily from would-be victims. When they do respond, it is often too little too late, resulting in yet one more homicide or other painful tragedy.

In stating these well-known and public facts, as is my right as an Australian citizen but more importantly as a victim myself of homicide, I don't mean to point the finger at well-meaning individual police officers. Unfortunately, we are all too familiar with the ongoing drill because we've heard it time and time again. The police department is far too busy to be making repeated house calls in order to keep alleged acts of violence under control.

They also have a specific code governing their responses and more often than not plausible explanations as to why they don't bother responding. These include insufficient manpower. Or "more important" crimes on their radar. Or lack of sufficient communication between emergency personnel taking calls and officers out on patrol. Besides, the jails are packed to the rafters. Where are the courts supposed to put the offenders? Much easier to save taxpayers money and let the offenders roam free following a brief court hearing.

The point I'm making is that most police officers are doing their utmost to see justice done. But even with the best of intentions, the outcome often doesn't rest with them. It's up to the judicial system to carry out sentencing, which is often more lenient than it should be due to budget constraints. This has created a vicious cycle that gives both victims and offenders the impression a human life isn't worth the effort. Especially since offenders who display even a hint of remorse often get off with a good-behaviour bond and are released back into the community, free to re-offend. When is the law going to change in favour of the victims?

Starting a Movement

I may be new at this, but I recognise the importance of raising public awareness about these horrific crimes against humanity. Perhaps we could use something similar to the Me-Too movement that has empowered people to speak up against sexual harassment or assault. I truly believe this could become a life-changing movement for women and children affected by domestic violence as well. I look at this cause as an assignment from God to make others aware of the seriousness of this escalating crime situation.

But I also know I can't do this alone, so I'm sending an SOS to anyone out there with the connections and power to move mountains for this cause. If the many organisations and individuals motivated by domestic violence tragedies will just join forces and form a single body with one goal in mind to stop these unnecessary crimes, we can end this senseless violence in our society. Yes, there are facilities in place right now, but not enough or such crimes wouldn't keep happening so frequently.

What I'm trying to say here is that we must be prepared to think outside the box about ways to help others in critical times. I understand it's hard to know just how to go about helping a cause like this. It's so much easier to step into defensive mode and decide not to get involved. But personally, I'm not a quitter, and the thought of not giving it my best shot has never sat well with me.

And the good news is that we're not alone in carrying out this urgent mission. We have a mighty hand reaching out to help us. God's mighty right hand, in fact, as the Bible promises us.

Though I walk in the midst of trouble, you [God] preserve my life. You stretch out your hand against the anger of my foes; with your right hand you save me. (Psalm 138:7)

It was not by their sword that they won the land, nor did their arm bring them victory; it was your [God] right hand, your arm . . . for you loved them. (Psalm 44:3)

For I am the LORD, your God, who takes hold of your right hand and says to you, do not fear; I will help you. (Isaiah 41:13)

Our God is all knowing, all powerful, always in our midst, and He is simply waiting to offer us His helping hand if we will just take it. How good is that?

So when it comes to this sickness getting out of hand in our society, let's not just "learn to live with it." Instead, let's work together as one to stop it before it spreads like the Covid-19 pandemic we're all having to deal with right now. It is a huge task that will take a great amount of courage and determination to accomplish. But that simply means we need to act on it now. Leaving for tomorrow what we can do today just doesn't cut it.

So let's all be peacocks instead of geese. Instead of sitting on our feathers, let's get to our feet and spread out our plumage to bring attention to this great cause. Let's raise our voices as one loud, clear noise instead of sitting in silence and fear. Let's come together as one nation and one movement to put an end once and for all to the horrible crime of domestic violence.

5

Let Go And Let God

As I'm writing this, I can hear God gently telling me, "Don't let your frustration get the better of you or pour out your anger on innocent bystanders who don't have anything to do with how you are personally feeling. You are doing your bit by stirring the pot of awareness through this project. Now I've got this. So just let go of it and let Me deal with the outcome.

Wow! If I know my God as I believe I do, then it's a done deal. He will make it happen in His time. My problem is that I want it now.

But as we all know, that's the way life happens. We have to calm down and display a certain amount of patience because throwing a temper tantrum (or as we say Down Under, "spitting one's dummy") and demanding that things happen according to our timetables doesn't work as far as God is concerned. Things will come to pass, but we have to trust His judgement as to when that happens.

That said, God always comes to the party when it's important to us, and I know that now. What I mean by this is that God already knows what's troubling us and how we feel. Even if things happen according to His timetable, He doesn't just leave us on our own until then. He will always respond to our call for help and point us in the right direction if we will just trust Him and not our own cleverness as the following scripture makes clear.

Trust in the Lord with all your heart and lean not on your own understanding; In all your ways acknowledge Him, and He shall direct your paths. (Proverbs 3:5-6, NKJV)

I love this scripture so much that I've memorised it and often recite it out loud at any given moment for no particular reason other than confirmation of God's Word and because I enjoy chatting with my heavenly Father throughout my day. God doesn't often answer me in audible words (though as mentioned in *Hidden Thorns* and my previous mention of my experience when recovering from tongue cancer, He sometimes does!). But I always know He's listening, and that comforts me immensely. The peace that engulfs my being is indescribable.

There is only one word that fits this phenomenon: awesome! It is a word I'm only comfortable using when describing God Almighty, though it is thrown around so casually in modern society. God is Spirit, and I readily admit I get as much pleasure communicating with God in spirit as I would chatting to my best friend on the phone. I love talking to God because it invariably turns my sadness into spontaneous joy. Now that has to be good for the soul!

It isn't just with my heavenly Father that I find myself chatting in spirit. Those of us who have lost a loved one as a result of domestic violence are often left wrestling in the aftermath with why it happened. A kind of guilt is often associated with such afterthoughts as "if only I ..." or "I'm sorry I didn't ..." We may appear to have things all together on the outside. But on the inside we are still thinking of our loss no matter how many years have passed and the "might-have-beens" if our loved one was still with us.

Even fifteen years later, there is not a single day in my life that I don't think of my Michelle and ask myself how life would have been if she was still with us. I even "see" her while watching television and in random advertisements. And, no, I'm not hallucinating as my husband made the same remarks about one particular ad where I could have sworn that the person featured was my daughter.

So while it may somewhat surprise you, I hope you will understand when I say that I still talk to my daughter in spirit. Of course, it's always a one-way conversation. These often take place when I'm having a bad-hair day and just happen to lay eyes on one of Michelle's photographs on display around our home. Our chats mostly go along the following lines ...

Hey, girlie! So much has changed since you've been gone. You should take a look at me now. I've changed. I love you so much! I wish I could see you one more time or even just talk to you in person. Alas, there are no visiting hours where you are, so even if I had your number, the angel in charge wouldn't put me through. If by divine intervention, he was to weaken due to all the love sent up and let me talk to you, there is still no way he'd allow me to visit even for a second. "Out of reach" is what he'd say. "No visitors permitted." But it's not going to be like this for-ever. How do I know that? The Bible tells me so, and mothers know best, right? So rest in peace, my darling one, because we will meet up again in Paradise to be re-united for eternity. That's a promise you can count on because God said so!

While I very much realise nothing will bring my daughter back to this life on earth, talking to Michelle in spirit helps me deal with the times when it becomes a little too hard to bear. Sometimes it's still not enough. I start thinking of grandchildren I'll never have with all their giggles and happy moments. Or other bright, sunny imaginary experiences I will never actually know.

On those occasions, it feels as if my soul is being lulled into a coma-tose state as though I'm permanently stuck in a solar eclipse, waiting in some frozen time loop for the sunlight to burst out and illuminate my world once again. In this hazy, dreamlike transitional state of mind, you don't have full thoughts or experiences but can still feel pain.

You may be thinking right now, especially if you've never lost a child, "Haven't you had enough time to get over your loss? It's been almost fifteen years!"

To which I would swiftly respond, "You can't ever put a time frame to this kind of a loss."

In truth, everyone's life journey is a very unique experience, and the effect of losing a child is also tailor-made to each individual. I've heard people say in response to the well-known "grass is always greener" proverb that the grass isn't actually greener on the other side of the fence. It's just a trick of the light. In fact, when it comes to dealing with the pain and grief of loss, we need to realise there is no trick of the light. The grass looks greener on the other side because God sends plenty of sunshine and regular rainfalls from above at the right time and in the right season.

In other words, there's a light at the end of the tunnel for all of us, and that's something to hold on to, right? So when I find myself floating in the comatose state of a solar eclipse, I kick into survival mode. I reach for my imaginary rope that will allow me to climb out of my frozen time loop and beyond the eclipse to let the light through. That rope is my lifeline, and my lifeline is my faith.

There is a phrase used to describe sunlight filtering through thick foliage so that it creates a pattern of light amidst the dark shadows: "puddles of sunshine." I love this imagery because when I get to feeling that grass is "greener on the other side," I can remind myself of who is sending those puddles of sunshine into my shadows, my loving heavenly Father. Which in turn reminds me how much better and healthier it is to focus on the "light puddles" instead of the shadows.

The author of the New Testament book of Hebrews describes faith as being confident of things hoped for and having assurance of what I don't see.

> *Now faith is confidence in what we hope for and assurance about what we do not see … And without faith it is impossible to please God because anyone who comes to him must believe that he exists and that he rewards those who earnestly seek him. (Hebrews 11:1, 6)*

In other words, perceiving as real what is not yet revealed to my senses such as having absolute confidence my daughter is alive, well, and happy in heaven with my Saviour even though I can only speak to her in spirit. In the meantime, I need to allow God to steer me in the direction He wants me to follow and trust that all those things I so desperately want to happen now will come to fruition in His perfect timing. Which includes being reunited with my precious daughter for all eternity when He finally calls me home.

6

Peace Of Mind

*“ You will find peace not by trying to escape your
problems but by confronting them courageously.
You will find peace not in denial but in victory.
~ J. Donald Walter ”*

Your mind is like an airport, and one's thoughts are like aeroplanes flying overhead, is a quote commonly ascribed to Greek Orthodox patriarch Elder Paisios of Mount Athos monastery in Greece (1924-1994). "If you ignore them, there is no problem. They will continue on their way. But if you pay attention to them, you are creating an airport inside your head and permitting them to land.

To put these words into perspective, let's imagine a busy airport where the control tower is finding the traffic increasingly difficult to handle, causing pilots to circle for longer periods than expected. In this imaginary airport, let's also assume the air traffic controllers are giving the pilots landing clearances on parallel runways simultaneously. Nor is anyone double-checking that these aircraft have not only landed safely but cleared their runways before clearing another aircraft to land on that same runway. Just imagine the mayhem both for the airplanes and in the control tower that will result from such actions.

While this is thankfully just an imaginary scenario, it's quite plausible to what has been actually known to happen in aviation over the decades.

You only have to watch television shows like Air Crash Investigations to understand the nitty-gritty of it. Those of us who fly routinely understand that operations within a busy control tower can be extremely stressful. So how does one prevent such situations from actually resulting in disaster when air traffic controllers are being called on to juggle many landings simultaneously, especially at peak times of traffic?

The solution is surprisingly simple and is in effect in aviation throughout the world. Those who work in the air traffic control towers must be totally focused on the job at hand. Any distractions that would be permissible in other jobs are prohibited. Controllers have to pass rigorous mental and personality requirements. They must take precautions to maintain health, and many commonly prescribed medications are banned because they could affect concentration. They are also trained to focus on precise communication. They have to demonstrate calmness and good decision-making under pressure.

Why? Because having negative or confused thoughts or lack of focus of any kind taking over one's mind while directing pilots to land and take off can put the safety of countless lives at risk. To put it simply, when you are in charge of other people's lives, it's vital to be at peace.

Have you ever looked up the meaning of the word peace and what emanates from achieving it? I have and find it fascinating. Peace means that you are in control of the situation in which you find yourself. It is a stress-free state of security and calmness, generally classified into two types: internal peace and external peace. I think you would agree with me that we need both of these. In a social sense, peace is commonly thought of as a lack of conflict and freedom from fear.

But more than that, to be at peace transcends the voluntary act to stop fretting about what may happen tomorrow because tomorrow will take care of itself. In fact, this is an instruction from Jesus Himself (Matthew 6:34). How do we do that? Just as the air traffic controllers must focus solely on the task at hand and be careful that everything in their life is keeping them from the distractions of stress and confusion, so the Bible tells us how we can maintain a mind that is completely at peace instead of anxious and fretting about all our present and future problems.

> *Therefore I tell you, do not worry about your life, what you will eat or drink; or about your body, what you will wear. Is not life more than food, and the body more than clothes? Look at the birds of the air; they do not sow or reap or store away in barns, and yet your heavenly Father feeds them. Are you not much more valuable than they? … But seek first his [God's] kingdom and his righteousness, and all these things will be given to you as well. Therefore do not worry about tomorrow, for tomorrow will worry about itself. (Matthew 6:25-34)*

In other words, when we keep our focus on our heavenly Father and His righteousness, He will handle taking care of our needs and problems, including all those worries of tomorrow and the next day and the next we tend to fret about. That in turn allows us to live each day in a state of peace.

The writings of Christian author Diane Eble reflect her passion for helping people connect with God through their own stories and hear His voice. She observes on the topic of finding peace: "When God speaks, peace is the message. Never settle for any course that's not characterised by peace. It's not God."

Putting It into Practice

So how to put this into practice in my own life? Peace of mind is an unmistakable ability to enjoy each moment. It comes with a loss of interest in judging other people or interpreting the actions of others because it permits us to think and act spontaneously rather than based on past fears and unpleasant experiences. That in itself is very relaxing.

But knowing that relaxation is far better for my health and actually acknowledging its benefits are two completely different ways of thinking. I tend to sit on the fence and look for the "what's next" in my life, getting on with whatever needs done rather than just enjoying the moment. Perhaps this is the reason my inner spirit has been giving me a gentle nudge now and then to deliberately set aside worry and take time to relax.

Of course, it's entirely up to me to be attentive to whatever message my inner voice is transmitting to my brain and act on it. When I do, I find that taking time to relax instead of worrying allows me to recover from stressful events. Furthermore, when I've had time to rest, my troubles gradually diminish and even dissipate completely. Bottom line, relaxation helps reduce anxiety, which is one of the biggest challenges people face throughout their lives.

After taking the initiative to let my hair down and relax for a while, I was amazed to find that it actually worked. It left me feeling much better within myself, which is certainly a good thing. I also realised I'd reached a stage in life where it suddenly became possible for me to take a back seat for once, a safe place where I could enjoy the ride without feeling the need to take control of the situation, which I would normally be inclined to do.

In short, my whole being needed decompression. This told me that my next step needed to be the refreshing of my soul, followed by the restoration of my mind. And the way to go to allow this to happen was just to sit back, relax, and let it be.

And so, I did!

7

God Given Talents

*Each of you should use whatever gift
you have received to serve others,
as faithful stewards of God's grace
in its various forms.* ~ 1 Peter 4:10-11

The term *God-given* typically refers to a talent or ability that is either innate—i.e., inborn, not learned—or is so extraordinary by normal human standards it could only have come from a higher power. A good example of a God-given talent is Mozart, who by age five was already composing complex pieces of music. A more recent example is Australian Olympian Jana Pitman, a world champion in track and field and the first female athlete to represent Australia at both summer and winter Olympics.

Another God-given talent is the human mind. Personally, I marvel at the similarities between the human mind and a computer's hard drive and motherboard. When my computer crashes, this is often due to errors in the operating system software or in the computer hardware. Software errors are more easily resolved. If I encounter an error within the software, I do my best to fix it and am successful most of the time.

In contrast, hardware errors can be harder to diagnose, hence their name (get it?). Okay, hardware actually refers to the physical components of a computer—the monitor, keyboard, central processor, etc.—while software is the operating system or coding a computer uses like Windows or MacOS. When I encounter a hardware problem, I may use a facility like "system restore" to reinstate what was lost. But this doesn't always work, leaving me with no other option than to call the fixer-upper, otherwise known as the "computer dude."

How good would it be if one could attempt to better the human mind in like fashion. Unfortunately, this is unknown territory and impossible to achieve due to its mechanism. We aren't speaking here about the physical brain contained in our skull. We are referencing the human mindset, which is altogether different and a great deal more complex, making it harder to diagnose. Just as with our computer, we must recognise the symptoms and act quickly if we are to understand its behaviour. That's when—you've guessed it—we need to get on the phone and make an appointment to see our doctor, quick smart!

Research shows that a majority of secular scientists and medical personnel believe the brain and mind are one and the same so can't be separated. But they most certainly can. The brain is a physical thing with several pounds of "grey matter," blood vessels, and nerve pathways giving it a definite shape (think hardware). As the centre of our nervous system, the brain coordinates our conscious movements, actions, and speech as well as unconscious functions of the body, whether sight, digestion, or movement of blood through our veins.

In contrast, the mind is a spiritual thing that cannot be touched or seen, yet its existence is evident by the "programs" of thought, feelings, creativity, memory, decision-making, and so many other intangibles it carries out (think software). It is the mind that gives us an understanding of "things unseen," including spiritual things, as well as a conscience that provides us with an innate framework of right and wrong, good and evil.

We know the brain has a specific location—inside the head. With regards to the mind, secular academics may claim it is located within the brain. But there is nothing measurable or tangible that can be pinpointed in a certain physical location and labelled as being the mind, giving it a sense of mystery. As I said, it's complicated and hard to wrap one's head around (excuse the pun!).

Sharing Your Gift with Others

Let's talk about the technical side of a computer, that being the field of expertise where I too am a "doctor," though without university diplomas bestowing letters such as MD, PhD, EdD, after my name. A little background here if you don't mind. From the earliest stages of my life, I became aware that God had kindly blessed me with a generous dose of common sense (which I've since found out isn't that common after all!). This gave me an ability to detect and fix problems because the solutions always seemed obvious to me, if not to others trying to find a solution.

Because of this, my workplace peers automatically called for me whenever someone had a computer problem they couldn't handle. I became known as the local "computer doctor" and even the "computer whisperer." Of course, my willingness and ability to help with workplace problems, primarily computer-related, was totally pro bono. Being of service to colleagues in their time of need gave me great joy and satisfaction. That said, there were times when I couldn't find a solution either, leaving me no option than to bail out and hand off the problem to the professionals.

This isn't intended to be a bragging session. In fact, just the opposite. Anyone who knows me well would vouch that I am always up for a challenge and will not readily quit until I've given it my all by hook or by crook. My personality comes in black or white with no room for grey, even though it's trendy to be greyish these days. Forget warm either as my opinion is always boiling hot or freezing cold. I am also most definitely a doer. It's all or nothing with me.

Being that kind of person has often worked in my favour because it allows me to take a good look at myself and recognise my own symptoms. This in turn has played a big part in my ability to discern the right time to connect my mind to my body so that my spirit is ready to commence its healing process at its own pace. Deep, isn't it?

Restoring the Mind

Today's generation isn't the first needing a restoration of the mind as the apostle Paul spoke of such a restoration and the results of having our minds restored.

> *And do not be conformed to this world, but be transformed by the renewing of your mind, that you may prove what is that good and acceptable and perfect will of God. (Romans 12:2)*

Renewing your mind is simply another way to describe restoring your mind. Now, I don't profess to know much about God's design for the human mind since that isn't a field where I can claim qualifications. But I can safely conclude in my humble opinion that the mind cannot restore itself while performing poorly. The mind is an amazing, complex work of divine craftsmanship that requires divine intervention to initiate its restoration so that it can once again reach its full potential. Our God is One who heals. But to do so, He wants us to grow closer to Him. As our relationship develops, so does the restoration of our minds.

How then do we come closer to God so that our minds can be restored? The Bible tells us that as well.

> *Since, then, you have been raised with Christ, set your hearts on things above, where Christ is, seated at the right hand of God. Set your **minds** on things above, not on earthly things ... since you have taken off your old self with its practices and have put on the new self, which is being **renewed** in knowledge ... Let the word of Christ dwell in you richly, teaching and admonishing one another in all wisdom. (Colossians 3:1-2,10,16)*

> *Finally, brothers and sisters, whatever is true, whatever is noble, whatever is right, whatever is pure, whatever is lovely, whatever is admirable—if anything is excellent or praiseworthy—think about such things. (Philippians 4:8)*
>
> *Put off your old self, which belongs to your former manner of life and is corrupt through deceitful desires, and to be **renewed in the spirit of your minds**, and to put on the new self, created after the likeness of God in true righteousness and holiness. (Ephesians 4:22-24, ESV)*
>
> *He [God] saved us, not because of righteous things we had done, but because of his mercy. He saved us through the washing of rebirth and **renewal by the Holy Spirit**. Titus 3:5*

So what can we learn from these scriptures as to how our minds can be restored? Here are several very simple and practical principles ...

- First, we need to focus our minds on Christ and those things that are heavenly and Christlike rather than negative things that can pull us down (Colossian 3:1; Philippians 4:8).
- Second, it is God's Holy Spirit who renews our minds (Titus 3:5).
- Third, our minds are renewed as we fill them with knowledge, specifically, knowledge of Christ and God's Word (3:10, 16).
- Finally, our minds are renewed as we put off our old self and ways that made up our lives before knowing Christ and put on a new self of true righteousness and holiness (Ephesians 4:22-24; Colossians 3:10). To understand the full contrast between what our old self looks like and what should be our new self in Christ and with minds renewed by the Holy Spirit, just read the remainder of these two passages (Ephesians 4:20-32; Colossian 3:1-17).

To receive this restoration of the mind, all we have to do is ask God, and He will give it to us (Matthew 7:7; James 1:5). The healing may be instantaneous, or it may be a process. That's entirely up to Him. Our part is to trust Him with thanksgiving for a work in progress. Because unlike a computer, there is no quick-fix formula for the human mind. You can't purchase a new one from Apple or anywhere else when the unexpected throws a spanner into the works, turning normality into confusion. Of course, this scenario varies from person to person. After all, our mindset is human, not machine.

For which I am deeply thankful as a computer or other machine may stay broken when smashed. But brokenness in the human mind, heart, or spirit can always be restored by seeking God's help through establishing an intimate relationship with Him and learning to listen to His whispers.

The best part is what our heavenly Father promises to us as we allow the Holy Spirit to renew and restore our minds. It may not be overnight, but we will find ourselves increasingly transformed into people who reflect Christ's image rather the sinful pattern of this world (Romans 12:2; Ephesians 4:24; Philippians 1:6). And we will find ourselves understanding and accomplishing God's good and perfect will for our lives (Romans 12:2).

8 |

Discerning God's Voice

The word discerning literally means hearing or listening. The ability to discern between good and bad can be quite challenging at the best of times. For me, total focus is imperative due to an ongoing physical condition called *tinnitus*, which is experienced as noises or ringing in the ears when no such external physical noise is present. Tinnitus is not a disease in itself but is symptomatic of a fault in the auditory system, which includes the ears and brain. You may have heard it referenced as "bells in your ears."

I have been battling these "bells" in my ears for years. This drives me crazy at times because they are ringing so loudly I can't even hear my own voice, much less those speaking around me. This can be awkward and even embarrassing, especially in public places where people feel compelled to shout when talking to me, undoubtedly muttering under their breath, "For goodness' sake, woman, why don't you get a hearing aid?"

This has become a constant battle for me as the bells never stop ringing. Only the volume seems to vary in tune with my blood pressure.

Some days are bearable while others can be rather difficult. But there is precious little one can do about this condition, so why worry about it? Does worrying help?

The obvious answer is *no* since worrying achieves nothing. The only way to cope is to pretend the bells aren't there, learn to live with the condition, and get on with life because that's the way we have to deal with so many things these days.

One additional obstacle I've experienced from this hearing impairment is that all the commotion of bells and whistles in my head makes it rather difficult to discern God's "still, small voice" (1 Kings 11:12). The good news is that if I can manage to hear Him with my condition, anyone can. But to do so, we must be willing to be calm, get into a quiet place, and be receptive to God's gentle whispers.

Being willing doesn't always come easy. In fact, it can become a mental battle, especially taking into consideration the circumstances and nature of what is troubling us in the moment. If I may be so bold, allow me to reiterate that the best way to rest our souls and rid ourselves of life's heavy burdens is by learning to hear God's voice. That in itself may require some extra concentration to begin with as discerning God's voice over all the other noises can be a bit confusing.

Allow me to elaborate here. First, there can be more than one voice in our heads clamouring for our attention with the aim of enticing us to follow them. These voices can be spiritual forces of evil (Ephesians 6:12) or our own wrong desires (James 1:12-15). It is easy to allow these voices to distract us from God's own small, still voice. And that, dear reader, will lead to disaster.

So how do we hear God's voice over all the other clamour in our heads? The best way to overcome this type of confusion is to master the art of having a discerning spirit, or mind, so that we may recognise the voice of our Good Shepherd, Jesus Christ. Pretence doesn't cut it because only His sheep know His voice just as our all-knowing Shepherd knows His sheep.

And when he [the Good Shepherd] brings out his own sheep, he goes before them; and the sheep follow him, for they know his voice . . . My [Jesus] sheep hear My voice, and I know them, and they follow Me. (John 10:4, 27, NKJV)

Learning to Listen

Learning to recognise God's voice isn't a skill that's acquired overnight because it isn't an innate ability within us. It is cultivated as God speaks to us at different times in different ways and in different settings (Hebrews 1:1-2). Let me share just a bit of how I have learned to cultivate a listening ear to discern God's quiet voice.

After a very active career working in the corporate sector, most of which was spent in the administrative side of business, I am now retired with my husband Stephen in Warwick, Queensland. Without a "nine to five" job to fill our days, we are cultivating the art of being content while waiting for God's next major move in our lives since we truly believe there remains one yet to unfold.

While retiring can be a reward for years of hard work, it can also trigger stress, anxiety, and depression. For me, this was aggravated by having undergone the loss of a child, since without constant activity to fill my days, I found myself once again dwelling on the loss of my relational sense of self as a mother. If I was no longer a career professional nor a mother, then who was I?

When one happens to be retired or works from home, as has become increasingly common since the Covid pandemic, daily life can become a rather monotonous routine even if we purposely arrange for busyness to keep the wheels of life moving day in and day out. We depend on unexpected happenings to break the monotony of our day and get our attention.

I am one of those people who indulge in one-on-one chats with themselves, and I know I'm not alone. When ideas become embroiled in my mind, I become confused to the point where I haven't got the faintest idea what I should do in the moment. My understanding of the situation tends to play tricks on me as I try to make sense of what's happening. Then the whole confusing feeling takes the form of a persistent inner voice that is continuously repeating the same message in my head.

That, dear reader, is when our ears should prick up and we know we must stop in our tracks to listen. Yes, that's right, listen! You see, when God has something important to say to us, He won't give up until we let Him have the floor. This is somewhat like a child tugging at Mummy's skirt to get her attention. But of course our heavenly Father uses reverse psychology with us because we're His children and He is our parent.

With that in mind, don't forget that God has all the time in the world to keep on tugging until we eventually stop what we're doing and listen to what He has to say. He knows all His children intimately because He has their names written on the palm of His hand (Isaiah 49:16). How awesome is that?

As we've already discussed, being able to hear what God has to say is an acquired gift. So it isn't always easy to do, especially when we are getting bombarded by all sorts of unexpected missiles hindering the "ears" of our hearts from listening. For me personally, hearing God's "whisper" tends to happen amidst the quiet surroundings of my study, which is also my "prayer closet" (Matthew 6:6) where I can shut the door behind me to be alone.

Once we stop and listen to God's whisper, He will in turn hear our pleas and petitions because a connection has been made. In computer terms, this means we are finally "online," our spirit to God's Spirit on air in the heavenly realm. That's it in a nutshell.

Ask, Seek, Knock

As we learn to discern God's voice, He in turn listens to our petitions. The key here is that we must be specific when we are requesting God's help. Though He already knows what we need, He still wants us to ask for it in order to deepen the bond between a heavenly Father and His child.

On a visit to Sydney prior to the age of Covid, I experienced a terrifying sensation while out shopping with my close friend Heather. All of a sudden, I couldn't see anything except dancing grains of light flashing and pulsating in the corners of my eyes. It's both disconcerting and annoying when it happens right out of the blue, leaving you to wonder if there's something wrong with your eyes, brain, or both.

If this has happened to you, the good news is that you're not crazy as I found out later from my optometrist. He explained that many people experience this phenomenon, and it had nothing to do with my eyesight in general but rather how visual pathways work inside the brain.

These distortions, otherwise known as a visual aura, usually precede a painful migraine, also referred to as an ocular migraine. Some people experience sensations of fatigue or nausea before it starts, but visual auras are among the most common signs. This can be quite scary if you don't know what it is as you may think you are going blind. But vision in the affected eye or eyes generally returns to normal within the hour in an ocular migraine.

While there are no drugs that specifically target this symptom, doctors will typically prescribe a migraine medication. Based on how badly one's vision is affected and what task one is performing when it happens, it may be necessary to make some serious lifestyle changes, especially in areas that require good eyesight. That's when it is important to seek God's guidance in prayer as to what to do next.

And so I did. In the end, I was left with no choice but to stop driving as my episodes couldn't be controlled. To even contemplate driving with this condition would be way too risky. The only treatment is resting when I experience one of these episodes, taking the necessary meds, and avoiding stress if possible as that only aggravates the situation.

While I understood the necessity, this drastic decision to quit driving altogether meant the complete loss of my independence. It took some time for the reality to sink in that I no longer had the freedom to go here, there, and everywhere as I chose. Thankfully, my beloved husband Stephen offered to drive me wherever I needed to go. That's actually pretty cool like being in a scene of *Driving Miss Daisy*, the 2014 film starring Jessica Tandy and Morgan Freeman as her chauffeur.

I don't tell this story to complain about one more health issue but to share that there is a solution for all our unexpected, hard-to-comprehend obstacles such as happened to me. We must be willing to listen, look up to the heavens, and ask God to intervene. When we ask Him to help us with our hurdles, we will receive because that is God's promise to us all. It might take longer than we anticipated, and the answer may not always be exactly as we imagined. But God's answer will be His absolute best for us and for our ultimate good, as God also promises.

> *And we know that all things work together for good to those who love God, to those who are the called according to His purpose. (Romans 8:28)*

But in order to receive, we must keep on asking. And if we are to find Him, we need to seek God intentionally as our opening verse above also promises (Matthew 7:8). To me, this beats any Help Line out there because you aren't just talking to mere mortals willing to listen to your troubles and give you the best advice they can. Instead, you are tapping into the very Source and Creator of humanity, God himself.

How good it is to know that we can connect to the heavenly realm whenever we are feeling tired and weary. In fact, Jesus graciously extends us an invitation in the Gospel of Matthew to come to Him whenever we are tired and struggling, assuring us that He will give us rest because His yoke is easy and His burden light.

> *Come to Me, all you who labour and are heavy laden, and I will give you rest. Take My yoke upon you and learn from Me, for I am gentle and lowly in heart, and you will find rest for your souls. For My yoke is easy and My burden is light. (Matthew 11:28-30, NKJV)*

I for one am grateful to be able to do just that. The sheer relief of knowing I can go to God and immediately download my ongoing burdens whenever I want without having to make an appointment or justify myself amazes me every time. This is the reason I keep on reaching out to Him because it's miraculously compelling. It's the moment we realise that God isn't there just to chasten us because we can't handle our own problems. He is there to listen attentively to our pleas and offer us His loving help in our time of need.

Once we grasp this overwhelming truth, nothing will stop us from continuing to seek God's help, especially as we become willing to listen to His still, small voice. And when we finally hear Him tenderly whispering in our ears the solution to our specific need, we will instantly be connected with Him through our receptive hearts. Faith is the passport we need to enter the realm of total peace of mind. I'm up for one of those! How about you?

The important key to keep in mind here is that the best way to connect intimately and effectively with God is to stop and listen. Once we are hearing God's precious whisper in our ears and hearts, the rest will fall into place since He alone can give us strength to carry on, and with that strength we can do all things in our Saviour's name.

I can do all things through Christ who strengthens me. (Philippians 4:13)

One other important key is brought out in our opening verse above. If you want God's door to be opened, you must make the effort to knock.

Knock and the door will be opened to you. For . . . to the one who knocks, the door will be opened. (Matthew 7:7-8)

No problem, project, decision, or move we're looking to make is too big or difficult for God to handle as He is all-knowing and all-powerful. Don't take my word for that. Check it out for yourselves in the Bible as there are many Scripture passages relating to this truth. The Bible also tells us that everything is possible for those who believe.

Jesus said to him, "If you can believe, all things are possible to him who believes." (Mark 9:23)

Assuredly, I [Jesus] say to you, if you have faith as a mustard seed, you will say to this mountain, "Move from here to there," and it will move; and nothing will be impossible for you. (Matthew 17:20)

Meaning that if we can't handle whatever life throws at us in the moment, we have the option of handing it over to God, who will take care of it on our behalf. How cool is that, and what more could anyone ask? I personally take solace in that promise whenever I am troubled. It's definitely worth a try because there's absolutely nothing to lose but oh so much to gain!

There are many inevitable givens in life, including suffering, pain, unfairness, and so on and so forth. When we experience suffering and pain, God wants us to knock on heaven's door and ask His Holy Spirit to quiet our mind so we can hear His still, small voice speaking words of love, peace, and wisdom while giving to our souls. All we must do is tune our hearts to pick up His messages, lay our requests before Him, then be ready to receive His abundant blessings. There's nothing more fulfilling than that in my humble opinion.

10

Perspective On Contentment

Be content with what you have;
rejoice in the way things are.
When you realize there is nothing lacking,
the whole world belongs to you.
~ Lao Tzu

Contentment is an emotional state of satisfaction that could be defined as a mental disposition drawn from being at ease in one's situation, body, and mind. This is a big task in anyone's agenda, let alone mine. But I'm determined to follow it through until I've reached my goal. I need to learn how to live again. This includes reacquainting myself with the world I live in, which is in many ways a place foreign to me due to the incomprehensible nightmare that hit me without warning like being struck at full speed by a London bus.

We often think of our circumstances as what determines the quality of our lives. Because of this, we pour our energy into trying to control every situation. We feel happy when things are going well. We are sad or frustrated when things don't turn out as we'd hoped. We rarely question how those two variables—our circumstances and our feelings—move in relation to the other. But in fact, it is possible to be content in any and every situation no matter how difficult, as the apostle Paul expresses so well.

> *I am not saying this because I am in need, for I have learned to be content whatever the circumstances. I know what it is to be in need, and I know what it is to have plenty. I have learned the secret of being content in any and every situation, whether well fed or hungry, whether living in plenty or in want. I can do all this through him [Christ] who gives me strength. (Philippians 4:11-13)*

> *Now godliness with contentment is great gain. For we brought nothing into this world, and it is certain we can carry nothing out. (1 Timothy 6:6-7)*

Contentment can help us distinguish between wants and needs. When we are content, we won't desire more than what we need because the abundance we already possess is enough to provide us with a happy, healthy life. Contentment often leads to the realisation that joy doesn't come from material things. I think an amen belongs here, don't you?

In fact, one excellent exercise to help foster a state of contentment is to intentionally reframe our thoughts by speaking them out into being as though we were having a chat with our best friend who only wants the very best for us. In other words, it's healthy to express contentment during difficult circumstances such as illness, relationship problems, bereavement, stress at work, etc. just as the apostle Paul did in his day. It worked for him, so why not give it a go?

That said, it is easier to say we should be content than to always feel contentment. This is because life has a habit of throwing in gritty moments that are hard to cope with at times. To understand how to deal a little better with such moments, let me pose the following question here. Do you have any idea how an oyster makes a pearl?

I've discovered that it is actually an extremely interesting process. It goes like this. When a grain of sand gets into an oyster's shell, this creates great irritation for the oyster. But instead of resisting and resenting the intrusion, the oyster does what comes naturally to it, which is to wrap the grain of sand in layer after layer of heavenly beauty, i.e., a lustrous crystalline material secreted by the oyster called *nacre*, or mother-of-pearl. In time, *et voilà*, a pearl is created.

The final lines of *The Oyster Poem*, written by an unknown poet, places this uncomfortable process into perspective beautifully.

> *And the small grain of sand that had bothered him so*
> *Was a beautiful pearl all richly aglow.*
> *Now this tale has a moral, for isn't it grand*
> *What an oyster can do with a morsel of sand?*
> *What couldn't we do if we'd only begin,*
> *With some of the things that get under our skin?*

Now that's something to think about since we've all got those gritty little things that invariably get under our skin. Things we have to deal with like it or not, so we must remember not to let the storm bury us under its debris. Meaning that if we keep our minds buoyant, our souls will become unsinkable. And, yes, there will be inevitable challenges along the way because time passes and life happens, leaving only memories behind.

To avoid going backwards while trying to keep the future in sight and learning to be content with our lot, we must train ourselves to recognise negative inner chatter the minute it starts because it has to be dealt with nonetheless. We may not always be ready to admit it actually happens. But guess what, it does! The good news is that there's a well-known and proven solution to this awkward situation, which is to mentally delete such negative thoughts the moment they start taking shape in our mind.

Sometimes it helps to make an actual "time out" signal with our hands as a physical reminder to ourselves. You might hesitate to try this in public lest your peers think you've lost your mind. But it does work, and no one is likely to judge you since many people meditate in such fashions, so why not at least give it a try. Be that as it may, whether you use a physical "time out" or just a mental one, any negative thought needs to be dealt with and ideally replaced immediately.

By this, I mean that we must reboot our minds and reprogram our way of thinking. Then bingo! We'll suddenly find ourselves on the right track and on top of the world looking at life through new eyes and rose-coloured glasses, thus enabling us to see hope on the horizon of our future. How good is that?

This is why it's so important to know that God is within reach so we can grab hold of the "rope of hope," hang on tight, and never let go for where there is hope, peace and joy usually follows. This is the contentment and acceptance of our circumstances that will become the next rainbow in our lives with all its adventures and blessings, waiting to be fully embraced when the time is right.

But for this to happen, we must restrain ourselves from trying to work things out on our own before God's timing and accept the limitations of living one day at a time. God knows our full capacity of what we can and cannot handle. When we follow His instructions with thanksgiving, we'll discover that everything in our lives falls into place at just the right time.

In other words, don't worry. Be happy!

11

A Life Worth Living

Stop and smell the roses is an idiom we've all probably heard at one time or another. Whether we take this advice as a literal act of admiring roses and breathing in their delicate perfume or as a metaphor, the core message is the same. We need to take time out of our busy schedules to relax, slow down, and just enjoy the beauty of life surrounding us. Of course, everyone has a different opinion and perspective on what constitutes a good life or how we should live our lives. For me personally, my life has held an abundance of blessings that have made it amply worth living. Admittedly, I've also had to face many challenges. But with God's precious whispers and the support of my loved ones, I've overcome them one by one and am a better person because of it.

The point I'm making here is that life is meant to be enjoyed, and when opportunities present themselves in whatever form they do, we should embrace them rather than feeling guilty about taking time for our own enjoyment. In fact, the Bible tells us that taking time to "smell the roses" is actually a gift from God.

> *There is a time for everything, and a season for every activity under the heavens . . .I know that there is nothing better for people than to be happy and to do good while they live. That each of them may eat and drink and find satisfaction in all their toil—this is the gift of God. (Ecclesiastes 3:1, 12-13, NIV)*

In other words, God gave us life to be enjoyed, not simply filled with toil 24/7 just so we can survive or even get rich. Of course, we all do have responsibilities, so it's also important to know when it's the right time or season "under the heavens." Since we don't get to decide what the future holds, we discover this by asking God for direction. He will give us our cue to take time out and smell the roses.

For Stephen and me, our time came in August 2015 when we decided to go on an overseas vacation beginning in Italy, the perfect romantic place to start smelling those roses, and ending in my beautiful country of origin, Portugal. Now, that's what I call living the good life!

The Italian experience was amazingly special because Stephen and I learned how to have fun without too much advance planning and with minimum fuss, which doesn't come naturally to either of us. We took a trip on Lake Como, which sits right at the base of the Alps in northern Italy. Along with snow-capped mountains and crystal-clear aquamarine lake water, our vista included an eighteenth-century villa belonging to the well-known American actor George Clooney. Sadly, major renovations were ongoing during our visit, so that view was spoiled by a flock of cranes—and not the kind with wings.

The Island of Capri just offshore in the Gulf of Naples was another gem of beauty. The highlight for me was our visit to the Grotta Azzurra, or Blue Cave, which blew us out of the water, excuse the pun! The bright azure colour of the water is due to sunlight entering the cave through an underwater cavity positioned below the entrance, which is itself barely wide and high enough for a small rowboat to pass through. As sunlight passes through the water, the red reflections are filtered out so that only the blue hue enters the cave itself.

Then there was the Marina Grande, a brief walk from our hotel along the beach, where Stephen conveniently lost himself one afternoon among the magnificent superyachts anchored there. We were looking forward to sharing a glass of bubbly with Australian billionaire James Packer and his then fiancée Mariah Carey, who'd been holidaying there on his luxurious yacht. But somehow, we didn't quite manage to cross paths. Ha, ha, ha!

Still, all good things must come to an end, and the time soon came to say *arrivederci* (goodbye; literally, until we meet again) to Italy and *olá* (hello) to my birth country of Portugal. This is one country where the familiar fragrance of roses spoke to me personally since my childhood nickname in Portuguese is *Rosinha*, which translates to Little Rose.

Stephen was keen to take in the scenery and learn the history of this magnificent country, which he'd somehow overlooked on previous trips to Europe before we were married. Maybe he'd just been waiting for his princess to come along, Little Rose from Portugal. How romantic! Judging by his reaction, he found it well worth the wait.

Needless to say, his experience wouldn't have been the same without me. Above all because he didn't speak Portuguese, and there I was ready to oblige. What a pleasure to be of assistance to my prince and show him the land of my birth. Being multilingual (English, French, Portuguese, Spanish, Italian) is a gift from God that has certainly come in handy. But if languages aren't practised regularly, they can become rusty, rather like the old adage "use it or lose it." So the key is to seize every opportunity to use them as losing them would be a shame.

A main purpose for this visit to Portugal was to introduce Stephen to our family homestead, Quinta do Pinheiral (Pine Forest Farm). My dad had inherited this sizeable farm from his father when my parents were still a young couple, and all seven of us kids were born there. Even after we moved to France and then Australia, they kept the property as a holiday home.

When Dad passed away in 1995, Mum couldn't bear the thought of selling the property, so it continued to be a holiday home for anyone in the extended family travelling to Portugal. As happened, I married Stephen less than a year later in 1996. Mum adored Stephen and looked forward to hosting him at the farm someday. But we'd somehow never gotten around to making the trip together before she too passed away in 2013.

That said, I'd often joined Mum when she was holidaying there with one or more of my siblings while Stephen held down the fort like a true gentleman back in Australia. Knowing how much it meant to me, he always encouraged me to go even when he couldn't, and I will be forever grateful for those precious memories.

Two of my siblings were already at the Quinta when we arrived, my brother Tony, who was also on holiday from Australia, and our oldest sister Alice, who lives in France. Reuniting there without Mum to welcome us as Lady of the Manor proved quite emotional for my siblings and me. We took time to remember her along with Dad and our dear brother John, who lost his battle with cancer in 2007, on a visit to our family crypt, where all three had been laid to rest.

The homestead itself is surrounded by field upon field of corn crops and grapevines. What sets it apart from other properties in the area is its unique entrance. The driveway leading into the estate resembles a tunnel of greenery, shadows, and light. This is actually an arched arbour comprised of stone pillars and wire mesh, over which numerous varieties of grapevines have been planted. During harvest season, visitors can alight from their car and choose among many delicious varieties to sample, a magical welcome for our guests. Once through the tunnel, visitors can see the original winepress in situ adjacent to a wine cellar where the product of our annual grape crop is stored in massive barrels to mature.

In its prime, our farm buzzed with activity as there were many kinds of fruit orchards to be pruned, livestock to be tended, and crops to be planted and harvested. Nowadays with farmhands being difficult to secure long-term, this much-loved property is barely paying its way outside of crop yields from the corn and grapes.

Even so, stepping inside our beloved Quinta again, especially being there for the first time with my husband, was epic. Stephen felt an immediate connection with our home as it is full of character. Typical of its era, it was built of sandstone, giving the home a warm, earthy, rustic look he liked. The inner walls of the original kitchen had turned completely black due to the smoke from its open fireplace. The oven was similar to those used for pizzas but much larger. To give an idea of its actual size, one of my older sisters, then in her teens, often hid inside the oven when playing hide-and-seek games with her siblings.

Of course, this was long after it was decommissioned. When my parents were first married, my grandparents lived in an upstairs apartment while my parents occupied the downstairs. After my dad inherited and my parents took over the farm, they moved into the upstairs apartment, where my dad built a much smaller oven. If I close my eyes, I can still savour the sweet, yeasty aroma and delicious, wholesome taste of Mum's rustic bread that emerged from that oven.

After Dad passed away, Mum decided to renovate the homestead, making it more liveable and contemporary while keeping the original building intact for memory's sake. A new wing was added with additional bedrooms and bathrooms as well as a brand-new kitchen, all built of materials and style to blend in with the original building. Mum's purpose in undertaking such a sizeable project was to accommodate the entire family when holidaying there, including spouses and children. Family closeness is one more thing that makes life worth living.

Though being here this time felt very different without the special magic only Mum could emanate to make us all feel at home. Mixed emotions engulfed me as I showed Stephen around because he'd never get the chance now to see the estate through Mum's eyes. How sad was that!

I know he'd have loved it as Mum was blessed with a wonderful gift of expression loaded with dollops of enthusiasm. When she told a story, her face lit up with an infectious smile while her emerald-green eyes dazzled like precious jewels, mesmerising her listeners and keeping them hanging on every word. In true Portuguese fashion, her hands moved as rapidly as her tongue when she spoke. Oh, what lovely memories I have tucked away in my heart!

Reflecting back on that wonderful trip—a rainbow amidst the cloudy sky of loss and grief I was experiencing at the time—makes my heart smile with happiness even now. The brilliant hues of that unforgettable rainbow were tailor-made for Stephen and me, leaving their imprint forever in our hearts. Wouldn't it be nice to find that perfect time and season to plan for another rainbow and smell the roses again?

Let me make clear here that I'm not suggesting we throw out the godly contentment and acceptance of what God permits in our lives we talked about in the last chapter. But God also gave us life to enjoy, and as He provides opportunity, there's nothing wrong with adding to our contentment and acceptance a zest of mystery and adventure to spice things up a little. We just need to be patient until God's perfect time becomes a done deal and *fait accompli* because He has made everything beautiful for its own time.

> *He [God] has made everything beautiful in its time. He has also set eternity in the human heart; yet no one can fathom what God has done from beginning to end. (Ecclesiastes 3:11)*

12 |

Precious Memories

So long as the memory of certain beloved friends
lives in my heart, I shall say that life is good.
~ Helen Keller

Yes, life is good, and I embrace it every morning when I wake up. Among those things that make life so priceless and worth living for me personally are memories of my country of origin and certain beloved friends we've left behind there. Memories are so precious and very much part of our lives. As such, they are there to be shared with others because they make us who we are. They are part of our whole identity.

Which is why sharing my country of origin and family heritage with you, dear reader, is so important to me. So let me offer just a few more precious memories before we return to Australia.

Portugal is a tiny country, but its Christian heritage has left it greatly blessed with countless churches. In the quaint country town of Famalicão where I was born, the essential buildings were all centred around the main plaza, including its historic Catholic church. In my childhood, all major town events such as baptisms, weddings, and funerals took place in this church. In fact, this was where my parents were married and where each of their seven little bundles of joy were baptised. Catholics practice infant baptism with holy water sprinkled or poured on the child's head by a priest invoking the Holy Trinity.

On our 2015 visit, the church looked as beautiful as I remembered but much smaller than my childhood memories. As is common in Portugal and all across Europe for that matter, the town cemetery can be found next to the church. These graveyards often have as much fascinating history as the churches. While my siblings and I visited the family crypt to pay our respects privately, Stephen wandered around, admiring the exquisite sculptures and ornate architecture. When he discovered a particularly impressive burial chamber with a sculpture of a lion sprawled across the top, his curiosity was immediately roused.

'Oh, that one!" I said when he asked me about it. "That's the crypt of a local count, Conde de Pindela, who was buried there in the early nineteenth century. Mum told us his amazing story when we were kids."

At Stephen's request, I went on to tell the story as Mum had told it to us. On a safari expedition to Africa, the count had rescued a lion cub. He brought the cub back to Portugal, where they became inseparable. When the count fell ill and subsequently died, the lion was so heartbroken he refused to eat. He was later found lying across the count's tomb, skeletally thin and a mere shadow of the majestic specimen he'd been. Touched by the lion's devotion, the count's family commissioned the sculpture to honour this rare love between man and beast.

My brother Tony had hired a car for this trip, so he became our tour guide, driving Alice, Stephen, and me to many local sights Mum had enjoyed visiting on her own annual holidays. We also made a point of catching up with some close family friends, another of my parents' rituals when visiting the estate and one we siblings continued out of respect.

Among those select people was my godmother's eldest daughter, who had founded a wedding venue business called Quinta Lago dos Cisnes, which translates to Swan Lake Estate. What makes this venue so popular is that it's situated in a renovated castle. The opulence and majesty of the castle and grounds make it the perfect setting for the fairy-tale wedding of every woman's dream.

As our hosts showed us around, they led us past a number of pig pens at the rear of the estate that had large coloured television sets affixed to their back wall. When we expressed our curiosity, our hosts explained that this was done purely to make the hogs happy and amuse the guests. If this seemed rather insane, it was apparently quite popular. And it was certainly unique as no one else had thought of having pigs as part of a wedding venue. Stephen and I had a lot of fun. Everyone was as happy as a pig in mud with a colour TV—ha, ha, ha!

During our stay, we also visited another of my godmother's daughters. She manufactures warm winter socks in a variety of colours, which she exports to many other countries throughout Europe. That's when Stephen had a "light bulb" moment. A friend of ours has a ministry that sponsors forty-five orphanages in Latvia and Ukraine. At this time, there was already conflict between Russia and the Ukraine following Russia's invasion of the Crimea and other Ukraine territories in February 2014. Little could we guess Russia would invade Ukraine again in February 2022. But Stephen made arrangements to facilitate a shipment of those lovely socks for the orphanage children by being the intermediary contact with our friend's ministry.

We were invited rather spur-of-the-moment to join the family for dinner. I take my hat off to the lady of the house for pulling off a scrumptious feast at such short notice. The *pièce de résistance* was Portugal's national dish, *bacalhau*, a succulent stew of layered salt cod, thinly sliced potatoes, hardboiled eggs, onions, olives, and other ingredients, all baked in the oven and guaranteed to create a symphony of happy notes between your taste buds and your saliva. Stephen was in his own food paradise and became a fan of *bacalhau* on the spot. What a night! Exquisite food and wine. Sublime company. What more could one ask for?

Now on to these two sisters' younger brother. Our respective families had been very close when I was growing up as our parents had known each other since their own school days. Because of this long-standing friendship, the younger brother made it a habit to invite over for a meal any family members holidaying at the farm on the eve of their departure. This time, Stephen and I were the ones leaving. Our farewell dinner went on until the wee hours of the morning, leaving everyone fully satisfied and happy for life was good.

We later visited another family whose daughter owns a sizeable T-shirt factory and who kindly gave Stephen and me a tour. We will always remember the generous hospitality these family friends showed us out of the love and respect they had for my parents. This gift of warm hospitality is one of many wonderful traits for which my beautiful country of origin is renowned and that visitors to Portugal, whether on holiday or a business trip, take away with them. For that, I couldn't be prouder.

Stephen and I finished our Portugal leg of our holiday in Lisbon, the capital of Portugal. Lisbon is among the planet's oldest cities, predating Rome, and the second-oldest European capital city after Athens. A typical feature of its buildings are the *azulejos*, or blue and white tiles, with which they are decorated. We enjoyed our time there like two children let loose in a fun park, exploring the city, going for walks along cobbled streets, and taking everything in.

But like those two kids in the park, our time to leave came far too soon with so much more left to see in this wonderful historical city. I wanted to plead like a child begging parents, "Please can we stay just a little longer?" But every holiday has to end sometime, and it was time for us to go home to Australia.

Speaking of which, another unique feature of Lisbon is a music genre called *fado*, which means fate. Known as the soul of Portuguese music, *fado* speaks to the harsh realities of everyday life, sometimes with a sense of resignation, other times with the hope of resolution. The music itself is beautiful but always melancholic. I'm kicking myself for not having introduced it to Stephen while there in the very city where it originated. But like Stephen's delayed first visit to Portugal, I'm sure there's a logical reason for this. It just means we have to go back and find time for another rainbow, right?

13

Love On Four Paws

Some people may find it hard to understand those of us who refer to our beloved pets—cats and dogs in particular—as children. But if you've ever had a dog or cat as a deeply loved part of your family, I'm sure you understand exactly what I mean. Especially pets who come along after our human children are all gone from the home. I shared in my last book of the unselfish, unconditional love I experienced from our three canine babies, Shadow, Mr. Biscuits, and Prince, all beautiful collies, and how that love helped comfort and heal me from the grief of losing my daughter.

But oh, how hard it was to lose these three precious canine "children" one after another. After losing our third collie, Prince, Stephen and I felt incapable for some time of moving forward due to all life had thrown at us. But in time, we began looking for another furry friend.

This proved a harder task than we anticipated just because of all the recurring emotions associated with loving and losing one canine baby after another. Since our last three babies had been collies and we were partial to that breed, we searched for a female collie in need of a loving home. But we had no success. Discouraged, we began wondering if we weren't meant to have another dog after all the grief involved with saying goodbye to our previous three furry friends.

Then one day Stephen came across an adorable male rescue puppy on Gumtree, a popular online marketplace. This interested us as our beloved Prince had also been a rescue, and we felt better about helping a living being in need, whether human or animal, over simply purchasing a puppy from a breeder. When Stephen saw his picture on the site, he immediately called me over. "Darling, I think I've found him. It's a Maltese Shih Tzu puppy wearing a blue jumper, and he is so cute!

I fell in love the moment I saw his little face. Stephen immediately contacted the owner to arrange a "meet and greet." We couldn't believe our luck when he turned out even cuter in real life. The little darling somehow knew in his tiny heart that we were there for him because he wouldn't stop wagging his tail to show his approval. It was a perfect match!

Needless to say, he came home with us that same day, sitting on my lap all the way home as he enjoyed his first car ride with his forever humans. Stephen and I were both as happy as two kids in a candy store with smiles from ear to ear. In God's great love, He'd given us another fur baby to lighten the load we'd been carrying and put that spring back in our step.

It's All in Their Eyes

At this point you're probably wondering, and rightly so, what on earth is so distinctive about a dog? About this dog in particular? Well, let me tell you. It's his eyes!

Eyes in any shape or form have always fascinated me. While their primary function is to give sight, they also have the power to reveal all kinds of emotion the moment they connect with another pair of eyes, human or animal. Hence the popular adage, "love at first sight." We are also told that our eyes are windows to our soul, and you may have heard someone referenced as "speaking with their eyes."

When small children look at you, they instinctively know what kind of human being you really are and can sense your emotions, whether you are well or ill, happy or sad. Words aren't needed because this kind of exchange is all executed through the eyes. This unique trait of communicating solely through the expressiveness of the eyes is commonly associated with children but even more so with animals because they don't have the luxury of expressing themselves orally.

Mind you, some dogs have a definitive way with their vocal cords that could be termed "doggie speak," which to me is just another language we humans need to master if we are to really understand our furry friends. But failing that, the eyes manage the job of communication quite effectively.

Being able to communicate with our eyes is a privilege that only comes from God, and those fortunate enough to be blessed with this rare gift have the power to make hearts melt and feel all gooey inside. Our precious little dog has it, and I don't consider myself biased in making that claim as others have also commented on his "speaking" eyes. He was introduced briefly in the last chapter of my first book, *Hidden Thorns*, but there is so much more to share about this little pooch, so I'm trusting you won't mind me giving him a few more pages in this sequel.

We chose Xavier as the name for our new fur baby, which suited his personality and looks—white, fluffy, and adorable—to a T. But that seemed a bit too formal, so he quickly became Bubba. Being so cuddly and the same basic size and weight of a newborn, I had the freedom to imagine in my Never Never Land of fantasy that I'd been sent this little creature to help fill the void of the grand-children I'll never have. If that sounds insane, I'm okay with it as it's all about feeling needed for all the right reasons, and I truly believe this sweet fur baby has been God's own provision to help me deal with my loss.

That said, it didn't take long for this little bundle of cuteness to make his mark in our household, and I can assure you it wasn't all lovey-dovey either! This includes chewing anything he could dig his sharp little fangs into when we weren't looking. In fact, if I had a dollar for everything he has destroyed over the past four years, I'd be a wealthy woman.

During his puppy stage especially, Bubba was so naughty we threatened several times to send him back to where he came from. Stephen would scold him sternly, saying, "If you keep this up, I'll take you back to jail!

Unfortunately, that did no good because he knew good and well we were kidding. Among his many misdeeds, Bubba is also a pro at ignoring what's being said when it suits him. I believe there's a name for that skill. Oh yes, selective hearing. Something we're all guilty of at one time or another.

Bubba is extremely cheeky and canny as well. He learned quickly that the only time we call him Xavier is when he's in trouble. When he hears that name, he runs for his life and hides under our bed where we can't reach him.

That got me thinking about a way to trick him. After all, we humans are supposedly smarter than our canines, right? If a woman can get to a man's heart through his stomach, I figured the same crafty skill could lure a little dog from hiding. It worked like a charm. To this day, just mentioning words he associates with food like breakfast, lunch, or dinner will draw out of his den.

Speaking of naughtiness, I saw a doggie T-shirt one day while shopping lettered with the words "Naughty is the New Nice". It was so apt I couldn't resist buying it, and I'm glad I did because Bubba looks adorable in it.

Admittedly, we knew full well from the start what we'd signed up for. But he looked so angelic we never imagined in a million years he'd turn out to be this mischievous. Looks can be deceiving, can't they! The closest comparison I can think of would be a tornado cleverly disguised as a loving white fluffy ball. But instead of disappearing as tornadoes do, this four-legged version will keep going until he runs out of adrenaline, upon which he makes a beeline for someone's lap.

Mine to be precise. After a couple of twirls to settle in and recharge his batteries, he looks up at me with those soulful eyes as if to say, "I love you." Instantly, my heart melts, and all his misdeeds are immediately forgotten—at least until the next time. Then right on cue, he magically slips into his doggie Lala Land of slumber.

Seriously, when someone is as cute as a button, they hold an instant passport to get away with just about anything, right? Master Xavier certainly knows the power he holds. He has clearly spent time examining himself in the mirror, cocking his little head from side to side and wagging his fan-like tail until he worked it out that this gave him carte blanche to get away with his tricks. Not to mention the pleading look in his gorgeous eyes that hypnotises us until all is given or forgiven. Talk about trickery!

We call this the Bubba technique, and yes, he has mastered it to perfection. Who would have thought we'd fall for it? I'm ashamed to admit I did hopelessly in an instant. Stephen tried to resist his manipulative ways. But he too was totally besotted with our Bubba and finally gave in to his antics. After all, they share the same hair colour and were born in the same month just three days apart. How's that for coincidence? Or should we call it a dog incidence?

Indeed, our eyes do reflect our moral character and inner emotions. In fact, Jesus Himself call the eyes the lamp of the body in His Sermon on the Mount, showing whether there is light or darkness within.

> *The lamp of the body is the eye. If therefore your eye is good, your whole body will be full of light. But if your eye is bad, your whole body will be full of darkness. If therefore the light that is in you is darkness, how great is that darkness! (Matthew 6:22-23, NKJV)*

What Jesus was saying in context is that if a person's heart and mind is filled with goodness, love, and other spiritual fruit, this will be reflected in a person's eyes. But a person filled with spiritual darkness will also reflect that darkness in their eyes even if they have a smile on their face. Bottom line, what you really feel and think on the inside will show itself in the expressiveness of your eyes no matter how you might try to conceal it—whether you are human or a mischievous fur baby named Bubba!

14

Healing From Heartache

Thank goodness Master Xavier is slowly mellowing as an adult dog. But at the best of times he's still a handful, keeping us on our toes. That said, he still gets his way most of the time because he's simply irresistible, and we lap it up whenever we can. It keeps us amused, and we all need more laughter in our lives, right? In fact, the Bible tells us that laughter and merriment are good for us and even healing medicine for our souls.

A merry heart does good like medicine, but a broken spirit dries the bones. (Proverbs 17:22)

Perhaps in reference to that Bible passage, it has often been said that laughter is the best medicine. Indeed, recent medical studies have demonstrated that laughter contributes to our physical, mental, emotional, and even spiritual well-being. If that is the case, then Stephen and I have earned an extension on life and healing from our losses because there are giggles aplenty and never a dull moment with Bubba in our home. As mischievous as he is, we couldn't contemplate life without him now.

Mind you, there are many occasions during the course of any given day when I could easily trade him in for a second bird to keep our singing canary company. I'm sure Birdie would rather have a lady friend in his cage to sing duets with him in sweet harmony rather than an annoying dog who barks at anything that moves. It would suit me too at times because this four-legged little creature certainly knows how to push my buttons!

All that aside, having Xavier has made a huge difference in our lives. Especially for me as I had a deep craving to be needed and more importantly for the company of a little one. I'm ever so grateful to Stephen for finding him when he did as I was growing more and more lonesome as time went by. It wasn't good for my health or his.

In fact, having a pet is definitely the best way I know to banish loneliness and eliminate depression. It is a win-win situation within anyone's reach. To begin with, it's an excellent way to keep fit and healthy physically as well as mentally. Stephen and I have such a good time when we take our fur baby for a walk, especially down to our main park in the middle of town.

Interacting with other dog lovers is also a benefit for dog parents as well as their canine children. It teaches our fur babies to socialise and teaches us to set boundaries while still having fun. It puts a smile on our faces and makes us glad to be alive as we exchange stories with total strangers who become acquaintances or even friends in the long run.

To be honest, there's no room for boredom or time to feel sorry for ourselves when we have a pet. Especially a dog because they have such a knack for bringing joy to our day even when life suddenly rains on our parade and all we want to do is to feel sorry for ourselves. This unconditional act of kindness is called love, and it comes straight from their little doggy hearts because they only want to see the best version of you. They have the ability to see right through any mask or armour you may have put on as a shield to fool others and to see the real you.

Long ago, someone pointed out to me that dog spells God backwards. I must say I found the comment a little odd at the time as I wouldn't dream of comparing the two. But having experienced a dog's unconditional love more than once in my life, I can better understand the comparison because God's love for us is also unconditional. He loves us whether or not we love Him back as the Bible reminds us.

> *This is love: not that we loved God, but that he loved us and sent his Son as an atoning sacrifice for our sins . . . We love because he first loved us. (1 John 4:10, 19)*

> *But God demonstrates His own love toward us, in that while we were still sinners, Christ died for us. (Romans 5:8)*

I've come to believe that God created dogs and gave them to us in part as an illustration of His undeserved, unconditional love. Human beings can be good or bad, kind or unkind, deserving or undeserving, rich or poor, followers of God or atheists, and their canine pet will still love them. There are few other living beings about whom we could say that—including other humans. What better reminder that our Creator loves us unconditionally and wants our love in return.

Addressing Separation Anxiety

The only draw-back in having such a loving dog as Bubba is that he is totally dependent upon us. This is wonderfully touching, but by the same token, we couldn't help feeling a little trapped when we wanted to go out. Bubba's behaviour was due to separation anxiety, which affects a lot of doggies and children too for that matter. Mind you, he did his best to pull at our heart strings, making it even harder for us to leave him.

Thankfully, we quickly fixed this wee problem by leaving Bubba with his groomer, whom he trusted and where he felt free to roam around socialising with other pooches. This kind lady did this for us as a favour whenever necessary and didn't even charge us. We called it his "kindy" as in kindergarten for dogs, and it worked a treat.

Luckily, Bubba's separation anxiety is all but a thing of the past as our little pooch has matured with age like a good bottle of red wine when well-cellared. So we can now do as we please without too much drama from our "little man." He's happy to be left with a treat in his playpen of sorts, which we lovingly refer to as his "pink palace"—pink being the only colour available when I purchased it online. Though he still makes a racket when we return home just to alert the neighbours to the arrival of his humans. Happy days!

Separation anxiety and accompanying loneliness are on the increase in humans as well as animals, and not just children. It can affect any age from the elderly to young singles living by themselves. Indeed, there have been reports of many people suffering from the condition during the long Covid lockdowns. Being physically separated from friends, colleagues, and family members with no clear end in sight has a significant impact on our wellbeing. When we are already restricted from visiting the usual people and places that bring us joy, we typically want to be physically close to those people with whom we share the deepest attachment. If this isn't possible, it can lead to feelings of disconnection, apathy, lack of self-esteem, and other unhealthy emotions.

In extreme cases, some individuals during this pandemic have become so needy for constant attention they've had to be constantly in the same room with their loved ones, even when sleeping, and involved in every activity of their daily lives. Their need to persistently hug and hold their loved ones close can also be quite intense. It just goes to show that separation anxiety in humans or animals cannot be ignored or it will get out of control and develop into something much, much worse.

This, dear reader, has become known as the "long COVID" syndrome, a form of anxiety developed after having contracted the virus. An ongoing illness like this, also referred to as "brain fog," can intensify existing issues within families. In other words, if there were mild anxiety disorders before the pandemic, these too often develop into something acute.

What can be done to help? Researchers have found that interactions with animals is highly recommended as this helps boost the immune system and also releases positive biochemicals in our brains and bodies. These interactions keep the humans and companion animals socially and emotionally engaged as well, another great benefit. In short, a loving pet, especially a dog, can help us stay healthy and happy in these uncertain times while providing an additional source of respite from our daily stressors, including separation anxiety. How good is that!

Having a dog in your world is not always easy or doable. But it's definitely worth considering as the advantages far outweigh the negatives. Among the many benefits mentioned above, it is also the perfect antidote to depression. Xavier gave me a reason to go on living when I was stuck in the middle of the tunnel unable to see the light at the end of it. A loving fur baby is God's gift to heal impossible heartache resulting from grief. A gift given because He cares about those who are hurting as King David expresses so poignantly in the Psalms.

> *The Lord is close to the brokenhearted and saves those who are crushed in spirit. (Psalms 34:18)*
>
> *He [God] heals the brokenhearted and binds up their wounds. (Psalms 147:3)*

15

Facing Fear Head On

Most of us have an irrational fear or two. Thankfully, for most people these fears are minor. When fears become so severe that they cause tremendous anxiety and interfere with normal life, they are called phobias. Unfortunately, I have one of those.

You see, sharing my faith with others through written words suits me perfectly. It feels natural for me to communicate this way rather than voicing my thoughts out loud. Oration has never been part of my skill set. In fact, I melt at the very thought of speaking in public as I fear I'll make a mess of things and face embarrassment. Especially if it means speaking in front of a bunch of people I've never met before.

When we're dealing with our fears, what is important to recognise is that sometimes all we can control is our own effort and attitude. When we put our energy into those things we can control, we'll be much more effective in what we do. Then we can celebrate our imperfections instead of beating ourselves up over them.

Recognising the Signs

Maybe you are thinking right now that even controlling your own attitudes and fears seems impossible. But let me assure you it can be done. How? The right mindset separates the person from the persona of fear and anxiety we too often deceive ourselves **is** who we are. This enables us to look at every obstacle with a can-do attitude rather than a cannot-do attitude.

Charismatic French-Australian celebrity chef Manu Feildel recently spoke about facing his fear while participating in the popular Aussie reality show *SAS Australia*. The show features various Aussie celebrities who take on a series of quasi-military physical and psychological tests administered by ex-Special Forces soldiers modelled after the SAS, or Special Air Service, which is the original elite British Special Forces unit. Feildel readily admitted to being terrified during the filming of the top-rating cooking series *My Kitchen Rules*, where he was a judge, for fear of messing it up. I would never have dreamed he was feeling such fear as he always seemed so comfortable in his own element, i.e., cooking. That, dear reader, is a classic example of recognising your fear and doing what it takes to conquer it. If not addressed in its early stages, fear has the potential to develop into an emotional depression for which there is no easy pill to take that will bring healing. The good news is that we can overcome our fears. We simply need to focus on that particular mindset by which we "control the uncontrollable," at least within our own attitudes and responses.

Let's face it, we live in a time of massive upheaval, which can be defined as a violent or sudden change or disruption to something. So many things are outside of our control, including how long the Covid-19 pandemic will last and how will the rest of the world react. That's a tough thing for anyone to consider or accept.

Many of us respond by searching the Internet for answers. But focussing on circumstances outside of our control won't get us anywhere, will it? It only contributes to feeling more anxious and overwhelmed. So when we feel ourselves getting caught up in fear of what might happen, we must try to shift our focus to things we can control. For instance, taking steps to reduce our own personal risk of catching the virus. Or even better, avoiding it altogether!

This is what I mean about having the right mindset. If we can't control the uncontrollable, there are various things we can do to ensure a right mindset, as we discussed in part in past chapters on restoring the mind and having an attitude of contentment. We can refuse to focus on the negative, including our fears and phobias, but deliberately focus our thoughts on the good and positive (Philippians 4:8; Colossians 3:1-2). We can take specific positive steps forward in areas we can control, including health precautions, regular prayer time and Bible study, and so much more. Most importantly, we can choose to leave those things we can't control in our heavenly Father's loving and very capable hands.

That said, no one can do this for us. We have to be willing to commit to this process of our own accord because we are the only ones who can control our own attitudes and responses, whether or not our circumstances seem quite uncontrollable. We also need to understand that fear is a "spirit" that does not come from God as the apostle Paul reminded his protégé Timothy.

> *God has not given us a spirit of fear, but of power and of love and of a sound mind. (2 Timothy 1:7)*

When we recognise that our fears don't come from God and that our heavenly Father wants to replace our fears with Holy Spirit power, love, and a mind that is clear-thinking, calm, and well-balanced, we will be far less likely to succumb to our phobias. I must concede I'm not quite there yet as I'm still very much a work in progress, figuring out how to become a little more like Jesus and a little less like me (Philippians 1:6). But let me share with you just one of those dreaded occasions when my own phobia seized hold of me and I simply froze.

The occasion was shortly after the release of my first book *Hidden Thorns*. Vision Christian Media, a popular inspirational radio station in Brisbane, invited me to do a podcast interview with their daytime broadcaster, whom I'd actually met years earlier through my husband, who was a business acquaintance. Though initially excited at the prospect, I quickly became a bundle of nerves as that unwelcome fear of public speaking crept up on me.

Why? Because fear is contagious, and if we listen to it long enough, we'll invariably get infected. The more I tried to ignore it, the stronger my phobia took hold to the point that I left the interview bewildered and disappointed. My mistake was in listening to the negative, i.e., my fear of speaking, where I should have been focussing on the positive. So instead of ending up with something wonderful to look back on down the track, it turned out to be just the opposite.

Don't get me wrong. For my interviewer and his listeners, the end result was great with the intended message and focal point successfully conveyed. But I must be honest that I had mixed emotions when the interview was finally over. I felt I'd let myself down as well as my host and audience, knowing I could have done so much better. Considering this all happened in the relative privacy of a radio broadcast studio, I can only imagine my panicky reaction if the podcast had been conducted in a different venue with a total stranger. No, let's not even go there!

Addressing The Uncontrollable Factor

I am not proud of my response back then in allowing fear to seize hold of me. But I also knew radio interviews were a great vehicle for sharing with the public my daughter's story and issues I was passionate about like domestic violence. And while I still felt fear (and have continued to feel it whenever I share my story in public), like celebrity chef Manu Feildel, I was able to control my attitude and response sufficiently that neither my host nor my audience had any idea of how much fear I was battling.

And despite my disappointment with myself, I am so glad I went through with the interview. If even one person's life was touched, healed, and/or pointed to God because I pushed through my phobia and shared my story, my heart will forever rejoice. In my humble opinion, there is nothing more satisfying than pointing others to God and healing. That is an absolute joy worthy of shouting from the rooftops.

Joy and hope are virtues that inspire strength to rise again. That said, finding strength to get up after a fall can be quite a task without those two emotions. Sometimes we simply need to rejoice even when we don't see anything that great to rejoice about as the apostle Paul also reminds us. In fact, it is a direct command from God.

> *Rejoice always, prays without ceasing, in everything give thanks; for this is the will of God in Christ Jesus for you. (1 Thessalonians 5:16-18)Rejoice in the Lord always.*
>
> *Again I will say, rejoice! . . . Be anxious for nothing, but in everything by prayer and supplication, with thanksgiving, let your requests be made known to God; and the peace of God, which surpasses all understanding, will guard your hearts and minds through Christ Jesus. (Philippians 4:4-6)*

When we rejoice in God with thanksgiving despite our circumstances, fears, and failures, such an attitude will promote success. And notice what the result is when we "control the uncontrollable" by rejoicing and giving thanks regardless of our outward situation. God replaces the phobias that are controlling our hearts and minds with His own immeasurable peace. We see this same assurance in the Psalms.

> *When anxiety was great within me, your [God] consolation brought me joy. (Psalm 94:19)*

As I see it, anxiety is a by-product of worry, and the devil is the chief architect behind our worries, doing everything in his power to steal joy, peace, and hope from us and making us doubt the strong foundation of our faith, which is Christ. This is when we must fight the good fight of faith (1 Timothy 6:12) and stand our ground against our adversary the devil and his forces of evil (Ephesians 6:10-13). Life's trials will no doubt frustrate us, but we must nevertheless exercise patience and wait upon God for His grace will sustain us and His joy will revive our soul (Psalm 23:3; Isaiah 40:31; 25:9). Now isn't that worth fighting for?

As I was saying, we need to share with others and celebrate big time when we experience victory—even if that victory seems small and insignificant at the time—because it's all about the joy we feel when our victory blesses others. This principle can be applied to my VCM podcast interview. That I agreed to do it despite my fear of public speaking still amazes me. And I feel it is worth celebrating this small triumph with you, my reader, because of the impact it had on those listening. It mattered to them, and this showed in their joyful responses.

Reflecting on that entire experience prompts me to share as well just why I was extra nervous that day. A couple days before the date on which my interview was originally scheduled, the podcast host called to ask if it was okay to postpone my interview for a week. The reason being that Franklin Graham, son of American evangelist Billy Graham and a well-known evangelist in his own right as well as president of Samaritan's Purse, would be arriving in Australia for a series of evangelistic campaigns. The only time he had available for an on-air interview was during the time slot originally allocated to me.

I was happy to accommodate their need since I was already deeply grateful for having been invited to do an interview with Vision Christian Media. Even more so because it was Franklin Graham's father Billy who led my husband Stephen to Christ at the first crusade Billy Graham ever held in Sydney, Australia, when Stephen was in his teens.

Still, this impromptu change was all that was needed for that dreaded fear to sneak in uninvited on the day of my rescheduled interview. After all, how would my inexperienced public speaking compare to the very same radio audience after they'd heard an interview with such a gifted Christian speaker and preacher as Franklin Graham? But though my self-confidence was shaken a little, I chose to exercise that "control the uncontrollable" over my phobia and get on top of this obstacle by claiming God's wonderful promise:

> *I can do all things through Christ who strengthens me. (Philippians 4:13)*

The take-away message here is simple. A life lived in fear is a life half lived, so don't waste any opportunity to live it to the full. In other words, take life as it comes and worry not because God's loving right hand will always be there to catch us if we fall as King David reminds us in the Psalms.

> *The Lord makes firm the steps of the one who delights in him; though he may stumble, he will not fall, for the Lord upholds him with his hand. (Psalm 37:23-24)*

16 |

Unexpected Curve Balls

In Australia, a country famous for its cricket prowess, a curveball is often known in sporting terms as a "leg spinner." In that respect, we Aussies are fortunate enough to have had one of the world's best cricketers representing us all over the planet. That outstanding athlete is none other than Shane Warne, known as the "king of spin." Sadly, Shane passed away unexpectedly from a heart attack at the age of fifty-three early this year. But he continues to be widely regarded as one of the greatest bowlers of all-time.

Shane was well known for his mastery of leg spin, delivering the ball time and time again with absolute precision. In effect, he caused the ball to deviate from a straight path by imparting incredible spin to it. Hence the terms "curveball" and "leg spin."

But for me and maybe you as well, curveball has another meaning. I'm referring to how the term is commonly used as something entering our lives that is totally unexpected, surprising, or disruptive. And typically not in a good way but something that has the power to develop into corruption and injustice.

That, dear reader, is what I'm struggling to comprehend and would like to discuss further with you if I may. I have been dealing recently with an unexpected life curveball in the area of trust and truth. What a beautiful world we'd have if everyone made a collective commitment to be completely truthful and trustworthy with each other. Unfortunately, that isn't the case and won't be until we are in God's eternal kingdom where there is no pain, grief, tears, or lies.

In the meantime, we must resign ourselves to the fact that some people choose to be deceitful and devious. Sadly, this has happened within my life network of acquaintances and colleagues, creating a chain reaction of events that left me feeling betrayed, helpless, and seriously out-of-pocket due to another person's deception. Why? Because one little white lie can open an avenue for more lies to follow and then create a web impossible to penetrate lest you destroy it completely.

Analysing The Possibilities

So what should we do when we discover that someone in our life has been intentionally dishonest? The best suggestion I can offer here is that we must resist the urge to let it slide by ignoring this evil behaviour. Staying silent doesn't honour us and won't do anything to help the disingenuous person.

We also need to ask ourselves exactly how this dishonest behaviour has affected us. Make no mistake, every deceitful transaction costs something, monetary or otherwise. But inflaming an already heated situation isn't the answer either. So before we fly off the handle, let's take a deep breath and consider our options.

You may ask, "Is it always a bad thing to get mad? Especially when our rights have been violated!"

I would respond, "No, it isn't because sometimes the problem that most infuriates us is one we are called to resolve regardless of the awkwardness it may create between the parties involved."

It's important to keep in mind that even well-deserved finger-pointing will put the other person on the defensive and perhaps stifle any constructive conversation we may wish to initiate in endeavouring to put matters right. That said, let's be clear here. If we suspect someone has lied to us or manipulated the truth, we're entitled to pursue the matter until we're satisfied with the outcome.

After all, those who traffic in deceit are often masters of scams that take great advantage of others, and their deceitful actions shouldn't be shrugged off. Especially when such people are portraying themselves as upstanding members of society and even the Christian community. When confronted, these individuals often try to cover up their deceit with another lie and then another. So it becomes our problem to determine whether the person involved is willing to come clean. Only if they take responsibility for their actions and are willing to make things right can the damaged trust possibly be restored.

Seeking Counsel

At this juncture, we may be tempted to ask a trusted friend to weigh in. But depending on the situation, that may not be a practical solution, especially if the conflict is with a mutual acquaintance and our friend may not want to take sides. So if that isn't an option, who can we turn to?

The good news is that there is Someone we can always turn to, our heavenly Father, because Scripture tells us God will never leave us or forsake us (Hebrews 13:5-6). Whether we're called to speak out against injustice, to forgive someone who's caused us distress, or are feeling intimidated because of another person's deceit, it is very comforting to know we can look to God for help because He will always have our backs.

The Bible also gives us practical principles for dealing with conflict when someone has wronged us, especially if that person is another church member or part of the Christian community. Matthew 18:15-17 and Titus 3:10-11 lay out three basic steps. First, go to the person directly and confront them as to the fault. If they won't listen, go back with two or three other Christians as witnesses. If that doesn't result in resolution, submit the problem to church leadership. If the person still refuses to make things right, you need to walk away and have nothing more to do with that person (Titus 3:11).

Bottom line, if we have doubts and misgivings about someone's trustworthiness, let's first ask God and then listen closely to what our hearts and heads are telling us. Dishonest people will sometimes try to turn the tables and make us out to be the ones with the problem, insisting that we're overreacting and reading things into their actions.

My advice is to not play along with that kind of manipulation because someone who has deceived us once is only too likely to do it again and again without so much as blinking an eye. Let me add here that one good way to deal with a dishonest person is to make sure we ourselves are being completely honest. If the other person doesn't know or care about our dedication to truthfulness, at least we can be assured of our own integrity before God and man.

In fact, the Bible makes clear that if we do what is right before God no matter what the wrong behaviour and deceit we may face from others, we will be blessed.

> *And whatever you do, do it heartily, as to the Lord and not to men, knowing that from the Lord you will receive the reward of the inheritance; for you serve the Lord Christ. (Colossians 3:23-24)*
>
> *But even if you should suffer for what is right, you are blessed. (1 Peter 3:14, NIV)*

The moral of this discussion is that if the other person isn't willing to speak truth, we must be prepared to stand fast and do what is right because that's the honourable thing to do, even if it means ending a long-lasting relationship. Truth is a powerful thing that will win out in the end as Jesus told His disciples:

> *Then you will know the truth, and the truth will set you free.*
> *(John 8:32, NIV)*

All in all, it comes down to our own integrity and the necessity of making right wrongdoings and deceit. You might ask, "What would Jesus do? What does God have to say about dishonesty and deception?"

I would respond that the Bible calls deceitful people "wicked" (Psalm 36:3; 43:1; Proverbs 11:18). In fact, deceit and lying are among the things Scripture tells us God hates the most (Proverbs 6:16-19). Of all people, one would think we could trust those claiming to be followers of Christ, right? But if integrity is not part of their character, my advice to go about righting a wrong is to lay the matter at the foot of the cross and let God deal with it His way. As our opening verse reminds us (Romans 12:19), vengeance is best left in God's wise hands, not ours. And that, dear reader, is good enough for me.

17

A Receptive Heart

Why do you go away? So that you can come back.
So that you can see the place
you came from with new eyes and extra colours.
And the people there see you differently, too.
Coming back to where you started is not the same
as never leaving. ~ Terry Pratchett

At the very beginning of our time together, dear reader, I spoke of aftermath in the context of surviving a catastrophe. For me, the loss of my only daughter Michelle. Trying to go on is so difficult and has only been possible through the healing love and strength of my heavenly Father. In truth, the era of predictable unpredictability is not going away. It's here to stay, and I might even call it my new normal.

But the term aftermath doesn't necessarily have a negative or sad connotation. It can also imply a period of growth and maturation that is birthed out of having to endure grief and trauma. I am reminded of what Joseph told his brothers after they'd sold him into slavery in Egypt and God used their betrayal to save not only his family but all of Egypt and surrounding nations from famine (Genesis 37-50).

You intended to harm me, but God intended it for good to accomplish what is now being done, the saving of many lives. (Genesis 50:20, NIV)

This promise is reiterated in the New Testament.

While nothing can change the reality of an evil man choosing to murder my precious daughter, I can look back over the years since and see how God has brought spiritual growth and healing in the aftermath of loss and grief, bringing me into a closer relationship with Him.

That said, as I've shared before, ramifications from traumatic events remain no matter how many years go by because the impact has been made and the damage has been done. There is no timeframe to when what we call the aftermath ever finally ends. It just gets a little more bearable over the years. Sometimes it's smooth sailing. Other times it can turn into a ferocious tornado at the blink of an eye. I use this analogy because tornadoes are extremely powerful. Imagine one engulfing your entire being, swirling you round and round as though in a dryer, then spitting you out to leave you motionless on its path of destruction like a discarded doll.

But unlike a tornado, the after-effects of extreme trauma never really dissipate, which makes rebuilding the devastation left behind more difficult and sometimes even impossible. So instead of trying to turn back the clock to what we once had, it is urgent that we focus our energy on trusting God and holding on to His hand when climbing our mountains and walking through our valleys, especially during times of vulnerability.

I will be honest that like Bubba I can be a bit selective of hearing when it comes to listening to my heavenly Parent. When we've been hurt, we tend to put up barriers. But we need to be very careful because a protective shell can quickly turn into a "heart of stone" (Ezekiel 11:19; 36:26), impenetrable and unreceptive. Invariably, we have it in our heads that an imaginary iron shield will protect us from more pain.

In reality, it may result in something more drastic such as closing the door to our feelings, which in turn can lead to shutting God out of our hearts, and we certainly don't want that!

Thankfully, my heavenly Father never tires of whispering lovingly to me, "Why don't you take My hand and walk with Me?"

He will keep at it continuously until I stop ignoring Him or pretending I didn't hear anything. These precious whispers have been ever so comforting to me and have played a significant part in restoring my mind since the loss of my Michelle.

So if I'm to go by what I've learned thus far, it's that God is love (1 John 4:8, 16) and that love can only emit from a soft heart. This, dear reader, is precisely what I'm working towards right now as I continue listening to God's precious whispers and hanging on to His strong, protective hand.

Which brings me to the most recent stage of my "aftermath." During the course of the year 2020, a series of significant events took place in my life. Experiences over which I had no control. These left me so that I had no other alternative but to pray and totally rely on God's grace. The lessons God taught me through these events are very much part of my period of growth and are applicable to whatever situation in which we might find ourselves when we have no idea of what to do next. Please bear with me as I share them with you.

A Brief Sea Change

God knows it's hard to learn how to appreciate difficult days and still be stimulated by all sorts of challenges as we journey through unknown and sometimes very rough terrain. So while the wheels of life did their thing, I was deeply thankful God brought more than enough unexpected events into my life sphere to keep me on the straight and narrow and ensure boredom would never set foot there.

This includes writing the book you are reading right now, a very important endeavour.

Another activity packed with delight and fun has been pottering in my garden. I decided organic vegetables were the way to go since research shows they are better for you and more economical in the long run. This wasn't something I'd ever ventured into, so it has been a pleasant surprise how much I've really enjoyed getting my hands dirty in my vegetable patch.

That was all well and good, but something was still missing. I couldn't quite put my finger on it, but despite my various distractions, I was feeling restless. Then the penny dropped.

A sea change! I realised. *That's what you need! A few days "me time" away from home just to recharge your batteries.*

A sea change for me automatically invoked Sydney, capital of New South Wales and homebase in Australia for our family since we arrived there in 1971. I'd lived there until 1997, and it was also where my daughter Michelle had grown up. Every time I fly to Sydney, I can feel the adrenalin kick in as the aircraft prepares for landing. When we touch down, I let out a sigh of relief and quietly whisper, "Oh my, it's so good to be home!"

My brother Tony, who never married, still lives in our old family home just two doors up from my sister Gloria's house. I always stay with him when I visit Sydney though it's quite emotional for me these days because of my own mixed bag of memories. Even as I'm typing these words, a sudden sadness engulfs me as invariably happens when I think of my loved ones who are no longer with us—Michelle, my parents, and my youngest brother John—and how happy we all were once upon a time in our old family dwelling.

But *que sera sera*, as we say in Portugal. What will be will be. The reality is that only God has the power to stop the wheels of life in their stride or change their predetermined course. If my sea change came to fruition, popping in to see my friend Heather, who also lives in Sydney, went without saying. I've shared before about what close friends we've been for almost fifty years. In fact, I've come to think of her as my adopted mother since my own passed away in 2013.

I believe God gives us certain friends by design, and Heather is certainly a gift from God in my life. I treasure the fact that she's always there for a chat when I'm feeling a little lost and need to download my emotions in order to refocus and move on. Let's face it, we all need that because it's vital to our well-being. When I talk to Heather, I forget what was ailing me in the first place, and sometimes that's all it takes.

So exciting times were definitely on the cards for my upcoming visit to Sydney. It had been three years since my last visit, and this one promised to be a much appreciated and long overdue tonic for the soul. Not to mention, an absolute blast seeing family and friends living there face to face again. If you haven't already guessed, I should reveal here that I'm a gregarious person who loves hugging. In fact, I truly believe there's nothing like a hug from a loved one to pump up one's spirit.

I always book flights well in advance in order to get the best airline deals available, so my arrangements were in place a good six months before my travel dates in February 2020. But just as I was packing with great anticipation for my departure, an unexpected foe reared its ugly head here in Australia and indeed across the planet—Covid-19.

18

Stormy Weather

Understandably, I felt rather apprehensive about going ahead with my existing travel arrangements. At the time, our nation's chief medical officers were of varied opinions about the magnitude or severity of the coronavirus, so travel was not yet restricted, and masks weren't mandatory. In hindsight, Australia and the rest of the world were much too complacent in how they handled this malicious strand, which sadly turned into a worldwide pandemic. But after much consideration, I decided to brave the risk, though I wore a mask at both airports and aboard the aircraft for extra protection.

Once I touched down in Sydney, I headed straight to Heather's home, which is just a fifteen-minute drive from the airport. I planned to stay a few days with her before heading to Tony's place for the remainder of my holiday. I couldn't wait to give her a hug and be welcomed by her beautiful smile. I've always thought there's something powerful about a person's smile, especially someone you know well. It carries with it the magic to make one feel warm and fuzzy inside, which is good for the soul at any given time.

Before unpacking, Heather and I sat down for a cuppa. At ninety-four years old, she looked as good as ever and hadn't lost any of the cheekiness in her twinkling gaze or smile. We talked non-stop like two schoolgirls having a giggle together about anything and everything. It felt like old times as Heather always goes out of her way to make me feel comfortable and ever so special.

But the next morning after breakfast, I felt suddenly unwell. I was experiencing a sharp pain in my abdomen such as I'd never experienced before in my life, and as you already know if you've read *Hidden Thorns*, I've had my share of pain! I did my best to conceal my increasing discomfort as I didn't want to worry my hostess. But Heather can read me like a book and quickly assessed the urgency of the situation. She suggested we make an appointment with her local doctor. I knew better than to protest and needed answers fast, so I gladly let her lead the way.

After a brief examination, her doctor prescribed medication for indigestion and reflux, but advised me to go straight to hospital if the pain persisted or worsened. We returned to Heather's place, but after another forty-five minutes, I couldn't put up a brave front any longer. If a picture paints a thousand words, as the adage goes, my face now drained of all colour undoubtedly told her everything she needed to know.

"Sweetheart, you don't look well at all," she told me with deep concern. "Why don't I call an ambulance and get you to hospital, quick smart!"

While she was on the phone, I called Stephen at home in Warwick to let him know what was happening. He supported Heather's swift reaction in calling an ambulance versus a "wait and see" approach. Too often in a situation like this away from home, we will go for the latter option when we are suddenly unwell just because we don't want to be a burden to our hosts.

In this case, I'd never experienced such pain and was naturally anxious to find out what was going on in my body. So I was thankful for the support in my decision to head to the hospital. Stephen also offered to call Tony and Gloria, my two siblings still living in Sydney, and to keep them in the loop as things progressed, leaving me free to deal with more pressing issues.

From Bad to Worse

I arrived at the hospital early evening. I was alone as I'd insisted Heather remain behind, not wanting to put her in any health risk at her age. The paramedics brought me into the emergency department (ED). That was when the chain reaction began with one bad thing happening after another to make an already bad situation worse.

First, there was total chaos due to the number of patients being brought in by ambulance because of the coronavirus. Though I'd come into the ED by ambulance, a female paramedic led me to the main reception area and instructed me to wait there until my name was called. Giving me a blanket, she added rather apologetically, "I'm sorry we had to come in this way, but we had no choice. It's not normally like this."

No kidding! I thought to myself. *Please get me out of here! I want to go home!*

Then my pain continued to worsen. When I was in enough agony to become desperate, I gathered the courage to walk over to the reception desk, my blanket still wrapped around my shoulders. Politely, I asked the duty nurse why I'd been made to wait here when I'd been delivered by ambulance to emergency. Coronavirus or not, I couldn't understand their logic.

Lifting her eyes from her work, the nurse responded without blinking an eye, "It doesn't matter how you came in, ma'am. Just look around. All these people have been waiting for hours. Whether they arrive by ambulance or not, every patient has to come through this check-in point because of the new virus. It's highly contagious, and the hospital has been inundated with people who have the symptoms. So go back to your seat and wait until your name is called out!"

For a split second when I heard those words, it felt like I was playing a role in a movie scene and didn't like what was happening. I wanted to ask the director to please rewind this film back to that feel-good airport scene where everything was unfolding beautifully and I was just about to have the best holiday ever with family and friends. Instead, the director tells me, "Sorry, there's no rewind button because this isn't a movie but real life."

Nurses tend to be compassionate human beings, and there was no doubt in my mind that this woman was simply overwhelmed by the sudden influx of patients and her consequent workload. But her words hit me like an icy blizzard on an already frosty morning. I stood there for a moment completely frozen, not sure how to react. Then without another word, I did a U-turn and returned to my seat.

Only to find it was now taken! I'd been told to go sit and wait, but now I literally had nowhere to do that. Walking across to one of several pillars in the room, I leaned against it, hoping it wouldn't take too long for another seat to become vacant. Thankfully, it didn't.

Four long hours into this nightmare, I was finally attended to in a small consulting room. The doctor apologised profusely for the wait and explained that the enormous incursion of patients was due to the new virus, already deemed to be far worse than the SARS (severe acute respiratory syndrome) virus that had caused so much panic back in 2002-2003. His consultation was brief, and I was once again told to wait, this time in a chilly corridor with dazzling-white fluorescent lighting.

Considering the lateness of the hour, the intense activity I saw everywhere projected a strong sense of panic. Doctors, nurses, and other staff rushed past to help people in need. But not one stopped to ask why I was kneeling on the corridor floor clutching my stomach, tears rolling down my face.

Then suddenly in the midst of this frantic traffic, I heard what sounded like music to my ears. "Are you all right? What's the matter? Is someone looking after you?"

Shaking my head, I sobbed even harder in despair. Glancing at my watch, I realised I'd been on my knees for more than an hour. Taking pity on me, this good Samaritan—doctor, nurse, hospital staff, who knows!— found a vacant consulting room equipped with a bed where

I could lie down to try and ease the pain until someone called my name again.

Time was meaningless as seconds ran into minutes and minutes into hours with nothing left to do but to wait indefinitely and pray. It is in moments like these when we truly come to the realisation that God really is within our midst, listening to our desperate pleas. This is a wonderful truth, dear reader, that can be adapted to any circumstance at any given time, not just hospital emergencies or other tribulations. All we have to do is to call on His name and believe He hears our petitions for that is His promise to us all (Psalm 145:18; Matthew 7:8; 1 John 5:15).

Long story short, I eventually found myself in the emergency department (ED), where under normal circumstances I would have been admitted immediately all those hours ago. Blood was drawn and a CT scan organised since the medical staff still didn't know what had caused the severe pain and nausea I'd been experiencing. Eventually, a doctor approached me with an encouraging smile as though she couldn't wait to relay some good news.

"Hi, I'm the doctor in charge of the ED, and I'm looking after you tonight. Your test results are back, and we're confident an obstruction of the bowel explains all your symptoms. This is like a knot forming in your intestines that blocks any movement. If there is no change, this condition could be extremely dangerous and even life-threatening. We have reason to believe it could have been caused by old scar tissue. Have you ever had an operation in the abdomen?"

I drowsily moaned an affirmative response. Nodding, the doctor continued, "What made you so ill earlier was a severe colic attack, which is when the gastrointestinal muscles contract around an obstruction. This requires immediate treatment to unblock your system. If that fails, we will have no other option but to operate. Any questions?"

Questions? I thought. *I've got a hundred of them, but do you have the time to listen?*

I wasn't totally convinced about it all as nothing had made much sense to me thus far. But with no other alternative, I shook my head in the negative. Since my case was now judged urgent, the nurses acted quickly, manoeuvring an oversized tube up my nose that went all the way down to my stomach. They apologised later that they'd run out of thinner tubes, which were easier to insert and therefore more comfortable, due to the influx of coronavirus patients. If the tubing wasn't painful enough, they also put me on an intravenous drip, which caused a great deal of discomfort after the many other needle jabs I'd already received that night.

Seriously! I demanded with silent desperation, looking at my bruised arm, which was now mottled red, blue, and purple. *How much more of this can I take?*

19

Miraculous Healing

I was eventually wheeled to the gastroenterology ward where a new team of doctors worked to unblock my intestines naturally so as to avoid surgery. That was when the penny finally dropped for me that this very strange trip to the hospital was going to be more than an overnight stay.

By now I was beyond tired. But lying down flat was an impossible task due to the agonising pain in my abdomen, which hadn't subsided even with the help of intravenous drugs.

I had to remain upright almost in a sitting position, and even that was more unbearable than awkward. The lack of sleep and pain had reduced me to an appalling state of mind, and as hours stretched into days, I truly felt my situation was hopeless.

I could only think of one thing to do—look up to the heavens and pray to my loving heavenly Father for divine healing. Or to put it more accurately, a miracle since that was the only way I could see out of the mess in which I found myself. In my desperation, I prayed and sobbed and prayed some more. I would have happily dropped down to my knees if that were at all possible. But my gut blockage and physical exhaustion put any such move out of bounds.

The medical staff, bless their hearts, kept trying various methods to fix my problem as they were reluctant to operate, though by that point I was practically begging them to do so every morning during their rounds. My belly had ballooned up in such a way that it felt as though I was about to give birth. In addition to that extreme discomfort, I'd been jabbed so many times in my right thigh (since other obstacles hindered injections on my left side) that the area had become inflamed, resulting in a hard subcutaneous lump the size of a golf ball that was very sore to touch.

Give me a break! I begged silently, trying to lull myself to sleep. *I don't need this! It's so painful!*

Concerned that my condition was so much worse than originally expected, Stephen wanted to drive down to be with me. But we had no one with whom to leave Bubba and Birdie, and I was still confident the blockage might be released at any time, upon which I'd be returning home. So I assured him I'd rather he hold the fort at home. In any case, there was nothing he could really do except talk to me and pray, and we continued doing this daily over the phone. What we definitely didn't count on was for my hospital stay to drag on day after day for almost two full weeks.

I found out later that the recommended treatment for an obstruction of the bowel hadn't quite worked the way it was intended because the "knot" in my intestines was gaining a tighter grip instead of relaxing. It eventually escalated to the point that I couldn't keep anything down, whether solids or liquids.

Flanked by his team of interns, the head surgeon finally informed me, "Marie-Rose, we're doing everything we can to prevent surgery because trust me, you don't want this operation if it can be avoided. But if your condition doesn't improve over the next twenty-four hours, you will be entering the critical phase, and we'll have no choice but to operate. So how about if we just wait and see. Are you okay with that?"

"Sure, let's wait and see," I responded. What else could I say? They were the doctors, and last time I checked, the doctors were the ones who got to decide what was best for their patients. So I didn't really feel I had any other choice, right? But what this medical staff didn't know was God's promise to never forsake or forget His children.

> *Be strong and courageous. Do not be afraid or terrified . . . The Lord himself goes before you and will be with you; he will never leave you nor forsake you. Do not be afraid; do not be discouraged. (Deuteronomy 31:6-8)*

> *As I [God] was with Moses, so I will be with you. I will not leave you nor forsake you . . . Have I not commanded you? Be strong and of good courage; do not be afraid, nor be dismayed, for the Lord your God is with you wherever you go. (Joshua 1:5, 9)*

And just as God promised, He didn't let this child—yours truly!—down. At the eleventh hour just before I was scheduled for surgery, He came to my rescue. I know He was there taking care of business because I'd reached that point of total helplessness where I was depending wholly on Him for divine healing. That, dear reader, is what God longs to see in us. That moment when we recognise no one else but His Spirit can help us get us out of the pit we're in and place our situation totally and trustingly in His divine hands.

In my case, even the doctors were astounded when the knotted section of bowel suddenly relaxed and straightened, permitting the blockage to leave my body naturally. Within a couple more days, my condition had improved to the extent that I was discharged. There you go, a classic example of prayer being answered—and I know many prayers were said on my behalf. More importantly, it was the healing miracle I'd asked God for in faith right in the midst of my worst desperation when I was feeling totally helpless.

Here is the great news. Prayer works! And it's there for all of us, including you. There's a very important message here I'd like to reinforce further. Never, ever give up even when things look grim or seemingly out of your hands. God's divine healing is within our reach today just as it was in the Old Testament when God healed through Elijah, Elisha, and the other prophets and in the New Testament when Jesus and the apostles performed so many miracles of healing. Here are just a few of the many promises of divine healing in Scripture.

> *"For I will restore health to you and heal you of your wounds," says the Lord. (Jeremiah 30:17)*
>
> *Bless the Lord, O my soul, and forget not all His benefits, Who forgives all your iniquities, Who heals all your diseases. (Psalm 103:2-3)Is anyone among you sick? Let them call the elders of the church to pray over them and anoint them with oil in the name of the Lord. And the prayer offered in faith will make the sick person well; the Lord will raise them up. If they have sinned, they will be forgiven. Therefore confess your sins to each other and pray for each other so that you may be healed. The prayer of a righteous person is powerful and effective. (James 5:14-16)*
>
> *Therefore I say to you, whatever things you ask when you pray, believe that you receive them, and you will have them. (Mark 11:24)*

In other words, all you have to do is ask and you will receive, provided it lines up with God's plans for your life (Romans 8:28). Why? Because God's timing is perfect, and He keeps all His promises. Amazing, huh?

During this impromptu tidal wave that almost swept me away into the storm, there was one ray of sunshine. To this point I'd received no visitors, though Heather, Stephen, and my two local siblings Gloria and Tony called often. I also knew they were praying for me. I understood their absence as every day we'd thought I'd soon be out, so coming in person didn't seem necessary. Especially since my siblings lived quite a long distance from the hospital on the far side of Sydney. But I felt very alone with no family around me.

Then one Sunday morning almost two weeks into my hospital stay, Heather surprised me with a greatly appreciated visit. That very afternoon, Gloria and Tony drove all the way across Sydney from the Eastern Suburbs to see me. I was over the moon to see all three of them but at the same time very much aware I didn't look my best. Since I couldn't keep anything down, I'd lost a lot of weight and to my eyes resembled a living skeleton.

But worrying about my appearance wouldn't help since the matter was totally out of my control. After all, I didn't have access to a make-up artist, and I certainly hadn't thought to bring such things with me because this was supposed to be just an overnight stay. So I chose to ignore my ego and enjoy these precious moments with my loved ones.

Bottom line, life happens whether we're prepared for it or not. When we find ourselves in this kind of situation, our appearance should be the last thing on our minds regardless of what visitors might think of us. After all, would anyone dare post pictures of a sick hospital patient on social media? Come to think of it, that might not be such a far-out thought these days! But I'd like to think those who take time to visit us when we're sick care only about who we are on the inside.

So that was some holiday! I must admit I felt rather cheated as I never envisaged in a million years that my lovely and well-deserved "sea change" would be spent in the hospital. Plus, I never did make it to my brother Tony's home to have my much-anticipated reunion with those family members who lived in Sydney.

I can say that this unexpected and difficult experience left me with a stronger sense of humility and immense gratitude to be alive and to be loved. A grateful heart is a loving heart. And a heart often becomes grateful because it has had experience in being ungrateful. This transformation from ungrateful to grateful only takes place when we realise how much there is to be grateful for despite life's trials.

Speaking of which, I had the privilege during this hospitalisation to nurture a brief friendship with a lady from Macedonia who was occupying the next bed to mine in our ward of six patients. We connected well and enjoyed an occasional laugh together that made our stay a little more pleasant and less lonesome. I can't speak for my new friend, but for myself, I was extremely grateful.

20 |

God's Mighty Hand

I was finally discharged from the hospital just one day before I was scheduled to fly back to Brisbane. Thankfully, Covid travel restrictions hadn't yet kicked in so I didn't miss my flight. When I touched down in Brisbane, Stephen and Bubba were waiting anxiously at the airport to take me home. How good is our God!

Having said that, I felt extremely fatigued after a so-called holiday I'd never had the opportunity to enjoy. Once home in Warwick, I did my best to settle back into my daily routine, which didn't prove as easy as I'd expected. Don't get me wrong here. I'm not lodging a complaint to the management up in heaven. I am well aware that no one is immune to life's challenges, and this kind of scenario could happen to anyone at any given time. In a nutshell, that's often the way the wind blows, and no one but God has the power to control it.

Still, what I'd thought would raise my spirits—my wonderful "sea change" of a trip to Sydney—ended up having the opposite effect. Which meant I was back to square one as far as my continued struggle with restlessness and feeling that something was missing. I'd barely been home a week when I suddenly felt a sharp pain in my chest. This quickly travelled to my left arm. At the same time, I was having trouble breathing.

At first, I wanted to dismiss my symptoms, assuming they were probably residual from my ordeal in Sydney. But the persistent pain began to concern me. That very day, Stephen already had an appointment with the chief medical practitioner of our local medical centre, so we made arrangements for a double appointment with him. This was a practical choice as the Covid-19 pandemic was now affecting every aspect of life. Medical appointments were being carried out at a patient's car in the rear section of the carpark just to cope with the influx of patients and concerns to keep the virus from spreading.

Unfortunately, we arrived at the medical centre to discover there was an ongoing emergency, so the doctor could only see Stephen. I was passed on to another doctor I'd never met before. He took my symptoms very seriously and arranged for numerous medical tests. Once he got the results, he immediately got on the phone to a cardiologist in Toowoomba, a city of about one hundred, thirty-five thousand population some seventy-five kilometres away. He then instructed me to go directly to St. Andrews Hospital there as they were expecting me.

Whoa! Hold on a second! I found myself thinking, completely stunned. I'd just returned from Sydney, where I'd spent most of my would-be holiday in the hospital. Now this young doctor I'd never met before was sending me off to a hospital in Toowoomba just like that? What was going on here?

But the doctor insisted it was necessary, so off to the hospital Stephen and I drove. I was even more stunned when the cardiologist in Toowoomba insisted on admitting me to the coronary care unit (CCU). I eventually discovered that both doctors were concerned I could be having a heart attack based on their examinations and my test results. After almost a full week in the hospital, my symptoms subsided. The medical staff in the cardiac ward admitted to being rather puzzled with my case. No surprises there as it seems to be that way everywhere I go!

While they couldn't figure out what might have caused my symptoms, the doctors finally concluded there was nothing physically wrong with me. On Friday afternoon, I was informed that my cardiologist had signed my discharge papers before leaving for the weekend and I'd be going home in the morning.

No one, myself included, considered for a moment that my trauma could be an ongoing aftermath of the events that had emotionally smashed my entire being to pieces in November 2007, nearly taking me down in the process. I came to realise that I was still struggling to let go of the hopelessness that had gradually taken over my ability to function after Michelle's death. I was now a broken vessel.

What do I mean by this? It's a growing awareness that no matter how hard we try to make things work, it only gets worse. And, unless we have God's intervention in our lives, it never will get better. Because of my brokenness, I'd allowed all those bottled-up emotions to mess with my mind since that fatal day.

Emotions of that intensity can't just be dismissed or erased from our minds but lie dormant like a volcano that hasn't erupted for a very long time but may erupt at any moment when least expected. The harder I tried to ignore them, the more persistent they became. Then one day, this emotional bubble just couldn't contain itself any longer and had to burst wide open just like the explosive pop of gas bubbles when a champagne cork pops. Out came all those mixed feelings with their ramifications, which included a serious physical impact on my body.

I'd been feeling somewhat better the last day or so since being admitted to the hospital a week earlier. But on Friday night, the pain came back with a vengeance. This time there was a numbness present, and I found breathing even more difficult than before my admission. It felt as though an elephant was sitting on my chest refusing to budge.

Understandably, alarm bells went off in my head, shouting, *Crikey! Something really weird is going on! I can't breathe, and there's a great deal of tingling happening on the left side of my body!*

I decided I'd better alert the nurse quickly. After I hit the call button, complete mayhem broke loose in my room. Buzzers were ringing. Nurses rushed in wheeling various types of equipment needed in an emergency situation to quickly ascertain the patient's condition. Fresh CT (computerised tomography) and MRI (magnetic resonance imaging) scans were done along with other tests.

As you can imagine, I never did get discharged the next morning. My cardiologist was astonished to come in Monday morning and find me still there. Looking somewhat baffled, he told me he distinctly remembered leaving the relevant discharge paperwork at the nurse's station on Friday before clocking off. But once he checked my new test results and ordered some additional tests, he came into my room for a serious tête-à-tête.

That's when he informed me I'd suffered a transient ischemic attack (TIA), often called a mini-stroke. This is a temporary blockage of blood flow to the brain. Because most TIA symptoms last from only a few minutes up to twenty-four hours, they are often not taken seriously. In fact, TIAs can be a forewarning of a major cardiac event, including fatal heart attacks. They can also result in ongoing consequences such as weakness, paralysis, problems with coordination, and slurred speech, not to mention leading to more serious strokes, heart attacks, and permanent brain damage.

The cardiologist immediately put me on a heart medication and blood thinner, which I will be taking indefinitely. I was enormously relieved to hear that all was well otherwise with no ongoing symptoms of the TIA. I was deeply thankful to have come out of this fresh health crisis intact, praise God!

More so, I realised how fortunate I'd been to be assigned to that young doctor when I'd been so disappointed the chief medical practitioner didn't have time to meet with me. If it weren't for his prompt action that day in taking the necessary measures to have me seen by the cardiologist, I may not be here to recount this story.

There is no doubt in my mind that this was once again God's mighty hand at work in my life and body.

More Stormy Weather

But wait, there's more! As follow-up to the mini-stroke, my cardiologist arranged for me to return to St. Andrews for a polysomnography. This is a comprehensive test used to diagnose sleep disorders that records brain waves, blood oxygen levels, heart rate, breathing, as well as eye and leg movements. While just an overnight stay, it was an extremely stressful experience I wouldn't undergo again if I can help it.

Then in December just when I was thinking 2020 was done with me, I found myself back at St. Andrews. Let me give you a bit of background as to how I once again ended up there. I told the story in *Hidden Thorns* of how my family moved from Portugal to France when I was quite young. I'm the youngest of seven children, and money was scarce for a big family like ours. Nor was oral hygiene strictly supervised with everyone's general busyness.

In consequence, by age sixteen one of my lower molars had begun to decay. One day it simply broke off, leaving me with a massive toothache. When I told my parents, they didn't seem overly concerned. For one, they incorrectly assumed it was one of my wisdom teeth.

"Don't worry about it," Mum told me with some impatience. "Everybody loses their wisdom teeth at some stage."

Now, don't get me wrong here. I will always love and respect my parents and certainly don't want to hop on the "blame game" wagon. When I was growing up, good dental care wasn't the given it is for most families today, at least in Australia. But I did think it a tad delinquent on their part not to pursue the matter further. Just saying, mums and dads, keep a watchful eye on your children's teeth.

As time went on and my moans increased, my parents finally took me to the local dentist. Shaking his head in disbelief, he removed the remainder of the tooth. He also informed my parents bluntly that it wasn't a wisdom tooth, and had they brought me in sooner, he might have been able to save it. As you can imagine, that didn't go down too well.

He then added: "We can look at options available to replace the tooth, or you can just leave it. My advice would be to think seriously about doing something sooner rather than later since your daughter is only sixteen and this tooth will have to be replaced eventually."

This put Mum and Dad in an awkward position, as they were already struggling to feed a family of nine and couldn't even consider such an unexpected expense. Needless to say, nothing further was done about it. On the positive side, I was young and otherwise healthy, so my mouth healed quickly, and the somewhat awkward gap in my teeth never really bothered me over the following decades.

That is, until recently. For a myriad of reasons over the last couple of years, I'd been wishing I hadn't lost that molar. For one, it had led to chewing problems and some other dental issues. Looking back, I have to admit I too was delinquent in not having replaced the molar early in my working career, so I have to offer a *mea culpa* here as well. But as the saying goes, there's no use crying over spilt milk.

In any case, I finally made the decision after much consideration to have a tooth implant done. The first stage had to be done in a hospital, so in December 2020, I was booked into St. Andrews Hospital in Toowoomba. By now you'd think I owned shares in the place!

The implant was a simple day surgery procedure, but I opted to stay overnight due to the travel distance from home and more importantly, though it was considered unlikely, any complications. All went as expected. I was back in the recovery unit, waiting until I'd regained full consciousness from the anaesthesia before being taken to my room. The nurse on duty called Stephen to advise him all was well so he could pick me up as arranged the next morning. But as you may already have guessed, all was not well. Within minutes of regaining consciousness, my heart started to beat really fast, and my blood pressure shot to alarming levels. My dental surgeon and his anaesthetist were immediately paged. I'd been their last patient for the day, so it was my good fortune they were still at the hospital.

I could see a worried look in their eyes, but the monitors were all behind me out of my sight, so I had no idea why. I'm thankful for that as had I seen what they were seeing on the monitors, i.e., that my vital signs were now in the danger zone, the shock alone might have given me a heart attack.

Not knowing what to do with me—again, no surprises there!—they paged my cardiologist, hoping he could shed some light on this unexpected emergency. In the midst of this confusion, I heard the anaesthetist say to the nurse, "Yes, I'll talk to her husband and fill him in on what's been happening. It's the least I can do as he's bound to be quite concerned."

Thankfully, the cardiologist was available to respond. He immediately instructed that I be moved to the intensive care unit (ICU) so I could be closely monitored throughout the night. As soon as they settled me in, I began to feel an unusual heat in my legs combined with an overwhelming urge to scratch. I assumed it must be due at least in part to the medical compression stockings I'd been provided to prevent blood clots from developing during surgery.

In addition, my mouth was packed with thick gauze and cotton pads to stop the bleeding from the implant procedure. I'd been given an icepack to hold against my cheek to help reduce the swelling. With all these obstacles, there was no way I could easily scratch myself, and the itching was driving me mad.

The nurses rubbed my legs to calm me down and try to alleviate the itchiness. By now my thighs were turning scarlet and looked like they were about to explode. I asked the nurses to remove my stockings, but they insisted it was too soon after the procedure. In the midst of this, I was again finding it difficult to breathe, so they affixed an oxygen mask on my face.

If that wasn't enough discomfort, I had wires stuck all over my body to monitor my heartbeat and other vitals. This left me lying flat on my back like an Egyptian mummy, unable to move or scratch. What a calamity! How had a simple dental procedure gone so wrong?

During the night, my legs suddenly contracted in unison with acute spasm-like cramps. This necessitated paging my cardiologist yet again as the nurses thought I was having some sort of seizure. I remained in ICU until morning, at which time I was transferred to a general ward for observation while this health puzzle was being assessed.

In the end, the joint conclusion of the medical personnel was that somewhere along the line I'd been administered in error a drug to which I was allergic, resulting in a similar violent reaction as someone with a serious allergy to bee stings or peanuts, for instance, might experience. Including hives, itching and redness as well as a closing off of the airways so that it was hard to breathe. I found this explanation a bit hard to comprehend given that all my allergies should already be listed in my hospital file. It's possible a drug was used I'd never been given before so there was no record that I was allergic to it.

Overall, I greatly appreciate the level of care doctors have towards their patients, and I'll never really know what happened on that occasion. All I know is that something went horribly wrong, and at the end of the day I'm still in the dark and none the wiser. On a more positive note, I'm happy to report that the second stage of the implant procedure has come and gone, also at St Andrew's Hospital, and all went according to plan, praise God. Instead of full anaesthesia, I received just a local anaesthesia, so no drama whatsoever.

What do I think about the whole process? Long story short, I found the implant worth all the effort, so I'm glad I had it done. There was one additional benefit to this nightmarish situation. My dental surgeon recommended I purchase a gadget unknown to me before this adventure called a Waterpik Water Flosser, which I promptly did.

Instead of dental floss, this gadget shoots a thin stream of pulsating high-pressure water to clean gums and between teeth. A definite must-have after a tooth implant or for overall dental hygiene. In fact, studies have shown this device to significantly reduce plaque build-up and gingivitis. At the end of the day, oral hygiene is vital for all of us, one reason I'm including this anecdote.

Going back to my original nightmare experience with this implant. Once again, I went in expecting an easy overnight stay and ended up at St. Andrews for the better part of a week. When my cardiologist finally discharged me, he had this to say.

"Well, Marie-Rose, here we are again! I have no idea how you ended up in my care this time when you were admitted for a tooth implant. Nor can I pinpoint just what happened to you after your surgery. The good news is that you're well enough to go home now. You're quite a puzzle to me, Marie-Rose, and for that I'm going to call you my Mystery Girl!"

Mystery Girl. It has a certain ring, don't you think? And I don't mind the accolade at all as it ties in nicely with what God has been doing in my life thus far. He is always there for me when it counts, which when you think about it is a kind of mystery in itself. After all, that is our heavenly Father's promise to all those who choose to follow in His steps.

The steps of a good man are ordered by the Lord, and He delights in his way. Though he fall, he shall not be utterly cast down; for the Lord upholds him with His hand. (Psalm 37:23-24)

22

Nature's Healing

It has been said that green is healing, bringing balance and harmony to mind and body. I'm in total agreement with that as many familiar herbs and garden plants were first grown for their medicinal uses and healing properties rather than taste or appearance. Since Stephen and I came to live in Warwick, I've discovered the healing power of one plant in particular that has made a huge difference to my well-being. Even while I was writing the previous chapter's implant anecdote, I sensed in my spirit that God was urging me to share this with you, my reader.

So how does God speak to me so specifically? Well, in this case an extraordinary sensation I was unable to control or explain suddenly took over, making it clear that I needed to pay attention now. It was as if someone was actually whispering so close to my ear it felt like a warm breeze blowing. The experience almost freaked me out because my study window was shut and the air-conditioning turned off. So where did this "draft" come from?

I felt lifted up to an almost trance-like state as though waiting for in-structions. That's when the warm breeze slowly became distinct words, the same precious whispers from God I've spoken of before. Above all, when God first told me verbally while I was recovering from tongue cancer surgery to write my story as I shared in *Hidden Thorns*.

"Walk with me, why don't you?" the soft voice said. "Close your eyes and let me bless you with My grace so that you can be a blessing to others through Me."

Closing my eyes, I thought, *What just happened? And how can I possibly do that?*

There was another warm, gentle breeze so near it was as though I was physically experiencing God's presence. Then I heard in my spirit another precious whisper. "Grace is sharing, so share."

A complete silence followed. Opening my eyes, I rubbed them, feeling as if I'd just woken up from a deep sleep. Still dazzled, I tried to make sense of what had just taken place as I was left stupefied by this surreal experience. God's words echoed in my mind for what seemed a long time as I attempted to process what had happened. Or had it been a dream?

Unable to rationalise my experience, I thought it best to just keep busy going about my day. That's when the penny finally dropped. God was encouraging me to share my own discovery with others whom it could bless. Isn't that what being gracious is all about? I'd say that showing we care about others by sharing God-given gifts with them is certainly right on the money when we are defining what grace entails.

To rewind a bit, all this started with a conversation I'd had with my dentist when I was having a crown put on. I have a long-term oral condition called *lichen planus*, which I've discovered isn't uncommon. It presents itself as tiny white dots, red swollen patches, or open sores that appear on the gums, tongue, or on the inside of the cheeks. It can be triggered by certain medications, a mouth injury, infection, autoimmune disorders, or even stress. Among the triggers are allergy-causing agents such as dental materials, including implants and associated products.

While not an ideal situation to find oneself in, *lichen planus* is manageable with medication. A common treatment dentists recommend is Kenalog, an over-the-counter corticosteroid ointment that temporarily relieves symptoms of mouth sores and pain. It had helped keep my condition under control, but I wanted to find a long-term alternative that didn't involve any pharmaceutical products.

Some years back, I'd made my annual visit to the oral specialist who had been dealing with my condition. I was eager to see if he'd notice any improvement in my gums. He seemed happy with his assessment but gave me a quizzical look. "Your condition is something of a mystery, Marie-Rose."

His words immediately sparked my curiosity since it wasn't the first time my health had been associated with the word mystery, as I shared in the last chapter. He went on, "Your mouth and gums are looking great. What exactly are you using to treat your lichen planus? Are you still applying Kenalog?"

"I'm glad you asked as I couldn't wait to see your reaction," I responded with a big smile. "I believe I've discovered something better than Kenalog."

"And what might that be?" he responded. "Please do tell as I've very interested."

"Aloe vera!" I announced with excitement.

Stephen and I had a planter full of the fleshy-skinned cactus-like plant in our garden. If you break open the long spikes, a clear, thick gooey liquid emerges. It has been popular historically for medical applications both topically and orally, above all as an ointment for burns, cuts, abrasions, and other skin conditions as the sap has anti-inflammatory properties that promote alleviate pain and healing.

I'd done extensive research on aloe vera clear back to my time as a beauty therapist and had discovered it is also packed with many vitamins and minerals vital for the effective function of all body systems, including antioxidant vitamins A, C, and E, and B12. Aloe vera has also become popular in juice form as the same anti-inflammatory properties have been shown to reduce irritable bowel syndrome and acid reflux.

I'd never heard of using the aloe vera plant to treat *lichen planus*. But if it helped skin injuries heal and could be consumed internally as a juice, then it made sense that applying this sap to the sores and redness in my mouth might also contribute to healing. In truth, I have no doubt the constant whispers in my mind urging me to try it could only have come from God. So I did.

I explained my findings to the specialist. "Every day after brushing my teeth, I carefully apply the aloe vera gel on to my gums, gently massaging it all over with a soft toothbrush as the area is extremely sensitive and can be very sore at times. I then swirl it around my mouth for a minute or two before spitting out any liquid. To achieve the best results, it's important not to rinse afterwards as that would nullify the benefits."

The specialist looked at me with astonishment. "What a marvellous idea! I would never have thought of that. Good for you for coming up with that alternative remedy, and my congratulations for being so diligent. It's clearly working for you, so keep up the good work."

That was the confirmation I needed to hear. The healing power of some plants and their medical applications is a gift God has placed on our planet to be discovered and shared with others so we can all reap its benefits. Aloe vera was healing my gums without the aid of pharmaceutical products, and that was good enough for me.

All went well with my newfound treatment until I decide to undertake the implant procedure in late 2020. When I told my dental surgeon of my discovery, he insisted I stop using the aloe vera. While I couldn't understand his logic, I obediently ceased using the aloe vera and resumed applying Kenalog to my gums. Almost immediately, I felt my gums flaring up again and becoming increasingly sore.

Thankfully, I had two scheduled appointments a fortnight apart with my local dentist to put on a crown, which is where this anecdote started. During her oral examination, she noticed my discomfort and the extreme redness.

"Are you still using Kenalog?" she asked.

Here we go again! I thought, shaking my head in the negative since her work in my mouth prevented me speaking. Once she finished, I explained about the aloe vera and how I'd stopped using it. To my surprise, she immediately suggested I discard the ointment and return to using the aloe vera.

Before wrapping up our session, the dentist took numerous pictures for her records. When I returned as scheduled two weeks later, she could hardly wait to see if my gums had improved. "How did you go with the aloe vera? Let's sit down and have a look."

After examining my gums, she exclaimed with great delight, "Oh my goodness! The improvement is amazing!"

When she compared my gums with the pictures taken two weeks earlier, I too became excited as the difference was clearly visible. The angry mouth ulcers had subsided, and the redness had all but disappeared. In fact, the dentist was so impressed with what she'd just seen she told me she'd like to recommend this natural treatment to others with *lichen planus*. Wow!

All this took me back to when I'd shared my discovery with the specialist all those years ago and how glad I'd been to pass on the benefits I'd enjoyed. I was even more excited to share it with my dentist as I have no doubt this can be a blessing to many others who have similar conditions. As I understand it, we're only scratching the surface of aloe vera's healing properties and other hidden benefits right now. Who knows what will emerge in the future as well as with other natural remedies we think of as ordinary garden plants.

For now, sharing with you, dear reader, what has greatly benefited me is enough of a heaven-sent gift for us all to enjoy. And if you don't have an aloe vera plant in your home or garden yet, they are easily and economically found at most garden supply outlets. Just food for thought!

23

Changing Seasons

For every human being from birth all the way through to death, one season succeeds another. This includes the various moods of nature with hot summers followed in due course by rainy seasons and cold winters. Springs and autumns have their own characteristics we all come to expect. At least for now since climate change is playing a huge role in weather patterns throughout our world. Thankfully, we can rejoice that God is still in control of the seasons and how they affect us all as individuals.

But there are also seasons of the heart. There are times in our lives when we are experiencing a heart season of pain. Other times we may be experiencing a heart season of joy. We spoke earlier, dear reader, of how the Bible tells us there is a time and season for everything (Ecclesiastes 3:1). This includes emotional seasons too, as King Solomon enumerates in this same passage.

> *There is a time for everything, and a season for every activity under the heavens . . . a time to weep and a time to laugh, a time to mourn and a time to dance. (Ecclesiastes 3:1, 4, NIV)*

We go through additional changes of seasons as we get older. For one, we become more sensitive to life in general. In my case, the awareness of God's message and guidance for my life through His tender precious whispers seems sharper and more in tune with each passing year.

That said, I think we can all be honest that we are never quite ready for life's metamorphic changes, the natural evolvement of time and seasons. As the years go by, we become so accustomed to our circumstances and routine we tend to linger where we feel most comfortable. We are even a little afraid of change because it disrupts our normal routines and makes our lives feel out of our control. We tend to feel more secure when our lives are predictable, so moving forward into the unknown can be frightening.

Regardless of our age, most human beings could be found guilty of thinking along these lines. Instead of accepting the challenge of something new as an exciting adventure, we bemoan the loss of our comfort. When a crisis does occur in our present-day lives—and it seems to do so when least expected—we let our minds wander into thinking we must be finished here and it's time to move on somewhere that provides escape from our circumstances.

But where? There! Where's there? Our safe escape could be anywhere, and not knowing becomes its own dilemma, locking us into a mindset where we are paralysed and again stuck because we don't know which way to move. So we wait as the phases in the mysterious volume of time take on different meaning, its chapters seeming to fly by right before our eyes, leaving us no time to enjoy the pages of life and embrace the changes within them.

But there is one change no human being on this planet has been able to ignore. Yes, you guessed it—the 2020 coronavirus pandemic. I have a descriptive alliteration of my own that I believe sums up well this global pestilence.

Power: Yes, it certainly has tons of that, though of the wrong kind.

Around: It went clear around the globe faster than any other virus.

New: It is debatable since there were other coronaviruses before Covid.

Deadly: While full statistics are unclear, it has killed countless millions.

Endless: It is still ongoing with no end in sight.

Menacing: It threatens humanity by constantly creating more variants.

Individual: Its symptoms vary greatly from person to person.

Cells: While vaccination controls the virus, no one is completely immune.

Scientists are predicting that Covid-19 will become endemic over time. This means the disease will still exist within the population but at a level that doesn't disrupt daily life, much like the common cold or seasonal flu rather than the global pandemic we saw in 2020. In the meantime, there may still be sporadic outbreaks, not just of a coronavirus variant, but other ugly viruses getting out of control like the most recent global scare, monkeypox. Yes, this is frustrating. But there's nothing we can do about it because, like the influenza virus, coronavirus, monkey pox, and who knows what other viruses are here to stay.

Interestingly, the Bible has quite a lot to say on this particular topic, and it's not sugar-coated either. It never is in Scripture because it's the truth. Many of us would prefer not to hear about end times because staying in denial is far more comfortable. But we can see the warning signs all around us just as Jesus predicted to His own disciples.

> *Now as He [Jesus] sat on the Mount of Olives, the disciples came to Him privately, saying, "Tell us, when will these things be? And what will be the sign of Your coming, and of the end of the age?" And Jesus answered . . . "You will hear of wars and rumours of wars. See that you are not troubled; for all these things must come to pass, but the end is not yet. For nation will rise against nation, and kingdom against kingdom. And there will be famines, pestilences, and earthquakes in various places . . . And this gospel of the kingdom will be preached in all the world as a witness to all the nations, and then the end will come." (Matthew 24:3-7, 14, NKJV; see full chapter; also Revelation 6-16)*

Through His loving whispers in Scripture and through the Holy Spirit to our hearts, God is giving us forewarning that everything is going to change. There won't just be wars, starvation, and pestilences, another name for pandemics, but also unprecedented natural disasters. We are certainly witnessing such disasters more frequently than ever before across the globe—earthquakes, fire storms, floods, hurricanes, tsunamis, tornadoes.

One of the worst tornadoes on record in the United States recently killed at least ninety people and left hundreds homeless in the state of Kentucky. Wildfires across western North America have destroyed hundreds of thousands of square miles of forest and burned entire neighbourhoods. Here in my own state of Queensland, the worst floods in decades affected several hundred thousand people in 2010 and 2011 and did over two billion dollars of damage. Only to be surpassed in May 2022 when even worse flooding allowed Stephen and me to once again boast of having a waterfront view from our Warwick hilltop despite living one hundred and forty kilometres inland from the ocean.

These mounting environmental catastrophes are signs that we are now living in the shadows of the Last Days. This makes sense because as a rule the shadow always precedes the body itself. Human beings as a whole are terrified by what they are seeing to the point that many of the wealthiest and most powerful personalities of our world are looking for a way out of Planet Earth, whether the so-called apocalypse-proof luxury bunkers purportedly built in New Zealand and the Rocky Mountains or an ark to the stars as certain billionaires are rumoured to be developing.

As it stands, no human being can predict when apocalypse will come or be able to avert its arrival as Jesus also told us clearly.

> *But about that day or hour no one knows, not even the angels in heaven, nor the Son, but only the Father . . .So you also must be ready, because the Son of Man will come at an hour when you do not expect him. (Matthew 24:36, 44)*

The message Jesus is laying out for us here is the importance of always being ready to face whatever is coming our way and to have the assurance of salvation through our Saviour Jesus Christ when that day comes. Because make no mistake, the end will come just as Jesus described. It's only a matter of when. If you want to know more about what can be expected in the end times, just read the last book of the Bible, the book of Revelations.

If this seems a troubling and even frightening topic, my reasoning in sharing this is that we must be ready for the unexpected but still remain hopeful. It isn't for nothing Australia is called "Land of the Holy Spirit" as discoverer Pedro Fernandez de Quiros first named this magnificent land in 1606. So fear not because God only has the best in mind for His children. Peace will reach our shores and dwell in our hearts once again.

Going back to those changing seasons we all must face, each of us is on a journey through life that is unique and special. Understanding the concept of change is a pathway into yesterday that casts a silhouette on tomorrow. The transitions we go through and how these impact our mindset and actions are what define the seasons of life. Just how long it takes to move through each season reflects our state of mind since no season lasts forever. Not the seasons of joy but thankfully not the seasons of grief or pain either. So if your current season of life is a difficult one, just hold onto your heavenly Father's hand, trusting that He will bring you through this season if you just have the patience to wait.

It all comes down to how we choose to look at our life, whether as a glass half-full or a glass half-empty, meanwhile reminding ourselves there are plenty of others who don't have a glass at all. The key is not to settle for a half-empty glass because it is the pessimist who always sees the glass as half-empty while the optimist sees the glass as half-full. Take your pick!

As for me, my glass is half-full, and I'm ready for a new season of change. Would you care to join me? Come on then, and let's go!

24 |

A Welcome Change

Let me give one caution here. Being excited about a new challenge or season of change shouldn't be license to charge headfirst into something we might later regret. As the adage goes, act in haste, repent at leisure.

How do we avoid finding ourselves in such a situation? We've spoken before about the urgency of seeking God's direction for every step along our life path. Everything God does is by His appointment and design, so nothing can come into our lives without His permission. This means we shouldn't get impatient if we feel something isn't happening quickly enough as it will definitely happen in God's appointed hour providing it is His will for our lives.

Unfortunately, we too often get impatient and find ourselves running ahead of God's plan. Making spur-of-the-moment, life-altering decisions without asking God first can be very damaging because there's a fine line between God-given assurance and self-sufficiency. When we cross that line, we must be prepared to face the music. At best, we risk delaying the fulfilment of God's perfect plan for our lives when we rush to get ahead of Him instead of asking for His direction.

I came across a well-known hymn, "What a Friend We Have in Jesus," written by nineteenth century preacher Joseph Scriven. The hymn speaks of the privilege of taking everything to God in prayer but also warns of the consequences when we don't:

> Oh, what peace we often forfeit.
> Oh, what needless pain we bear.
> All because we do not carry
> Everything to God in prayer.

Allow me to elaborate further on this point because Stephen and I found ourselves facing precisely this reality all because we failed to pray about everything before acting upon it. If you read my first book, *Hidden Thorns*, you may remember that we relocated to Warwick, Queensland, a country town of about fifteen thousand population, because we desperately needed a change of scenery in the aftermath of my daughter's murder. I can concede now that this move was part of a series of hasty decisions as a couple.

What started the ball rolling was our move from Sydney to the Gold Coast shortly after our wedding without praying about it or waiting for God's confirmation. As newly-weds, we were excited to explore all the yet-to-be-discovered treasures the Gold Coast had to offer. Known as the "Sunshine State" with all its contagious glitz and glamour, it felt much like living in Las Vegas, USA.

Then came our decision to flee from the Gold Coast to Warwick after Michelle's murder. Whether or not moving was the right decision, it could have been better planned and carried out with better thought-out timing. In truth, I wasn't in my right frame of mind during that extremely sad, stressful period and was simply frantic to leave the area where my only child had lost her life.

Regardless, both moves were very much make-it-happen-in-your-own-strength decisions. Thankfully, our God is merciful and can work out even the mistakes of those who love Him for our good and His purposes (Romans 8:28). And that included our time in Warwick. It took years of battling to understand why God has left us planted here in Warwick for the penny to finally drop.

Simply put, our God is a great, loving Father who knew Stephen and I had to deal with our massive grief and was keeping His children safe and away from potential harm. What better place to make a fresh beginning than a small country town far away from the dreaded crime scene where it all happened on the Gold Coast. In fact, living in semi-isolation here during Covid-19 proved a blessing in disguise because we were effectively cocooned from the pandemic.

Thank you, Father God, for looking after us even though we didn't understand Your real motives. And forgive us for whinging and complaining like children when things don't go their way.

That said, Stephen and I had assumed this season of country living would be a temporary one. By the time a full decade had gone by, we both felt the situation had gone on for far too long. Let's face it, the life clock was ticking, and neither of us were getting any younger. We were both missing city life, and the thought of living again by the seaside had become more and more appealing until we could almost taste the saltiness of the Gold Coast's beaches and ocean water.

Over the years we'd lived in Warwick, we'd made far too many decisions without consulting our higher authority for approval, simply charging ahead on our own accord. So when we decided the time was right to leave, we wrongly assumed our house would be quickly snapped up and we'd soon be living our dream somewhere on the coast. After all, our house ticked all the boxes. Great views on a hilltop. Sizable grounds. Beautiful gardens all around us.

But nothing happened. There were no buyers. Strange, huh? I've come to the conclusion that our heavenly Father definitely has a sense of humour, and He was just waiting for us to realise what we were forgetting in our eagerness to leave. For one, asking God's opinion on the matter. For another, that God's timing may not be ours.

Instead of asking God for advice, we ended up blaming each other, which only made matters worse. This reminds me of a Bible story about Moses, the great man of God who led the Israelites out of captivity in Egypt where they'd been slaves to Pharaoh. But his first attempt to be Israel's deliverer ended in disaster with Moses killing two men and fleeing into exile for forty years (Exodus 2). All because he'd charged ahead of God's timing and plan to deliver the Israelites, trying instead to do it by his own strength.

When Moses finally obeyed God's call at the burning bush to lead the Israelites through the wilderness to the Promised Land (Exodus 3), he had to face Pharaoh under dangerous circumstances ten different times. This time Moses persevered in faith and obedience to God because he could see the bigger picture and was prepared to step outside the box. Meanwhile, the Israelites whinged and complained whenever things didn't go their way, crying that they were better off in Egypt where they'd at least had food and water. The consequence of their rebellious, ungrateful attitude was that their entrance into the Promised Land was delayed another forty years.

All to say, when God whispers a message to our hearts, we must obey in faith even if the circumstances don't appear ideal for obedience. Rebelling will only delay God's blessings, thus prolonging the time to move on. The key for Stephen and me would have been to discuss our plans with God before going in "head down and tail up," which is exactly what we didn't do. Bad move!

Needless to say, however hard we tried to sell our house so we could leave this town where God had planted us in 2008 for His own good reasons, we simply couldn't find the right buyer. God's intent was to stop us in our tracks because He knew our hearts weren't in sync with His will. With reluctance, we eventually abandoned altogether any further attempts to sell our house.

How different things might have been if we'd taken the initiative to seek God's direction, wisdom, blessing, and advice before signing the contract on that house. That we didn't could be classified as rebellion and doing our own thing just like the Israelites in the wilderness. And just as the Israelites had to wait another forty years to enjoy their next exciting season as God's people, we are left with no option but to wait until God's right timing releases us to move on to whatever new season He has planned for us. Lesson learned!

You might ask, "And what exactly did you learn, pray tell?"

I would respond, "I'm more resilient and have quit worrying about tomorrow because tomorrow will become yesterday soon enough. I've also learned that in this life it's imperative to take time out of our busy-ness and smell the roses more frequently. Above all, I've learned that prayer is the master key of a blessed life for without it the doors along the way will remain shut and in turn steal the blessings intended for each one of us."

Acceptance in general is a defined skill and a hard one to maintain on an even keel, especially when stormy weather is rocking our boat, sending it adrift while we're desperately trying to reach our destination. Accepting our lot in life wherever God has placed us in the present moment is an ongoing process.

This, dear reader, is the exact point where I find myself right now whether I like it or not. Stephen and I are still patiently awaiting the green light from God's Head Office as confirmation to go ahead with our next move. In the meantime, I'm comfortable and happy to be where I am with Stephen, Bubba, and Birdie, our dear little yellow canary. But I also know there is a lot more life to be lived, umpteen places to be explored, and loads of moments to be enjoyed and shared with loved ones.

All of which tells me I'm now ready for the challenge of a new season of the heart, and I can vouch for Stephen as well. Where? Only God knows the answer to that question, and until He's ready to reveal the location, there's only one logical thing for us to do, which is simply to wait.

I can honestly say here that if there's one truly meaningful thing Stephen and I have learned during our Christian walk, it is that God always has a perfect plan, and everything happens in His timing, not ours. In learning this vital lesson, I've finally reached the point where I'm completely at peace with myself and content to be wherever God wants me to be at this point in His plan for me. As such, I've taken out a court order against rebellion and the "blame game," banning them from coming anywhere near my heart again.

The moral of this story is to never hurry God. We must try to be patient because good things come to those who wait for an answer to their prayers. Like the Bible says, there is a time and season for everything, and the time to move on will come soon enough. We just need to stop making that our focal point like the old adage "a watched pot never boils."

What really matters in the end is recognising that Mr. Impatience and Mrs. Anxiety are no longer welcome in our sphere. Instead, our focus should be to go about our lives, preferably with a smile on our faces, taking each day for what it is. A gift from God designed intentionally for the moment when He opens our eyes each morning. A gift of undeniable majesty wonderfully wrapped in heavenly scent and opening up slowly as the day unfolds before us. As we truly appreciate what an incredible gift we've been given, we can proclaim joyously with the psalmist:

This is the day the Lord has made; We will rejoice and be glad in it. (Psalm 118:24)

25

The Art Of Waiting

Patience is a virtue; possess it if you can.
Seldom found in woman, never found in man.
~ Anonymous

Exercising patience in order to restrain ourselves from complaining is a difficult skill to master as the second can't exist without the first. For me personally, learning to "bow down" graciously to my circumstances has definitely been a challenge since by temperament I want immediate answers to my questions.

Dare to imagine for a moment that I am a Minister sitting in the House of Representatives at the Australian Parliament House in Canberra. It is the open floor question time when politicians introduce their government bills for debate and voice their opinions. In this daring scenario, I step forward to address the House, determined to elicit a response from one if not all my political colleagues on the following question.

"Mister Speaker, the issue here today is that I need answers as I have absolutely no idea in which direction our party is moving, let alone when this move is going to happen. Can someone in the House enlighten me, please?"

Okay, I'm being a bit flippant here, but isn't it healthy to have a laugh at our own expense once in a while? The point I'm making is that exercising patience doesn't come easily when we find ourselves with little or no indication on our radar as to which direction to take in the immediate future. It's one thing to exercise patience when we're simply waiting for something we're excitedly looking forward to arriving. For instance, that big holiday trip we've scheduled or a visit to loved ones (okay, neither of those are all that certain either, as you've seen!).

Existing in limbo with no idea how long we need to be patient or what we are being patient about is far more difficult. But as children of God, that isn't necessarily a negative because living in a period of uncertainty as we await a decision can also be defined as synchronising with God's will. Meaning we need to pray about everything and totally rely upon God's direction rather than leaning on our own understanding and jumping the gun to make the decision ourselves as King Solomon advises us so wisely.

> *Trust in the Lord with all your heart and lean not on your own understanding; In all your ways acknowledge Him, and He shall direct your paths. (Proverbs 3:5-6)*

A reminder that we don't need to know every fork and curve of the road ahead. We just need to trust the One who does. These periods of uncertainty may seem to us a season of isolation. But it is also a season of preparation to ready ourselves for the next step in our lives according to God's will, not ours. And when we submit to doing this God's way, He will respond like any loving parent when our time comes by directing our steps.

Meanwhile, having a better understanding of God's reasons behind what is happening in our lives makes the waiting more enjoyable. There is no better situation to be in than where God wants us, so we need to stay put until He gives clear direction to move or we'll miss out on His next blessing. This includes pouring heart and soul into the life God has given us now rather than focussing upon the uncertainty of the future or constantly trying to figure out what's next.

Choosing to live our day-to-day lives positively makes a big difference in how we see the road ahead even when we encounter some unexpected potholes. My beautiful Mum had the perfect attitude when something unexpected happened or life suddenly rained on her parade.

"Don't worry," she'd quickly say to us with her sweet smile. "Tomorrow is another day."

No matter how tempestuous the storm, she always had faith the sun would eventually shine again, and that endearing slogan made a significant difference to how I look at life. Without even realising whose adage I'm quoting, I often find myself uttering her very words. Though she is no longer with me in this world, I can still see her smiling at me, and I smile back at her in spirit to say, "Thanks, Mum!"

Jesus also gave us good advice about fretting over what lies ahead.

> *Therefore do not worry about tomorrow, for tomorrow will worry about itself. (Matthew 6:34)*

A Grateful Heart

Instead of worry or impatience for what lies ahead, the Bible makes clear that we need to come to God with a heart of gratitude and thanksgiving for all of His current blessings.

> *And be thankful . . . singing to God with gratitude in your hearts. (Colossians 3:15b-16)*

> *Give thanks in all circumstances; for this is God's will for you in Christ Jesus. (1 Thessalonians 5:18)*

> *Oh, give thanks to the Lord, for He is good! For His mercy endures forever. (Psalm 106:1)*

> *Giving thanks always for all things to God the Father in the name of our Lord Jesus Christ. (Ephesians 5:20)*

When I looked forward years ago to this present point in my life, I had very different expectations of where Stephen and I would be in our twilight years. I assumed it would be a time of sitting back and reflecting on the past, preferably with a contented smile on my face to indicate that life has been good. Children and grandchildren would be stopping by once in a while for a chat, coffee, or meal. An inviting scenario countless couples enjoy in retirement. Never did I expect to enter my twilight season feeling empty or, even worse, without any real purpose.

Thankfully, as I've realised I can do nothing about my immediate situation but wait, I've also finally come to accept the cards life has dealt me in the past and God's will for my future. This includes death as it too is part of life's cycle. And indeed for children of God, death is nothing to fear but a glorious future reunion with our Saviour and loved ones who have gone ahead. And while I still grieve when I think of what could have been, my heart is also filled with gratitude to my heavenly Father because I recognise that the life He has given me is a great one.

This is probably why I relate so well to the popular tagline the Aldi supermarket chain uses to promote its products in Australia: "Good. Different." Meaning that they may be a very different kind of retail grocery, but their products are as good as far more costly brand names. My life today is different from what I expected all those years ago. But it is also good in its own way, and I'm okay with that.

26

Tell Them About Me

The Easter celebrations of 2022 had just come and gone when I sensed one more precious whisper from my heavenly Father: "Tell them about Me."

I'd be happy to, Lord! I prayed silently. *But how do You propose I do it?*

Then it occurred to me that Easter is a mega-celebration worldwide as well as a time of reflection for most Christians. After all, it marks the resurrection of Jesus Christ who gave His life for us on the cross.

Perhaps some readers may ask, "So what if Jesus rose from the grave? How does that affect me?"

Allow me to explain it simply. The Bible tells us that we've all sinned and the penalty of sin is death. But Jesus paid the ultimate price on the cross for our sins and overcame death through His resurrection so we too could have eternal life with Him in heaven if we only place our faith in Him.

For all have sinned and fall short of the glory of God. (Romans 3:23)

> *For the wages of sin is death, but the gift of God is eternal life in Christ Jesus our Lord. (Romans 6:23)*

> *For what I received I passed on to you as of first importance: that Christ died for our sins according to the Scriptures, that he was buried, that he was raised on the third day according to the Scriptures. (1 Corinthians 15:3-4, NIV)*

> *For God so loved the world that He gave His only begotten Son, that whoever believes in Him should not perish but have everlasting life. (John 3:16; see also Acts 16:1; Romans 10:9-10)*

In other words, death is not final for those who have placed their faith in Jesus Christ. How good is that! If you've never done so and would like to secure your own place in heaven and let Jesus help you become the person God created you to be, you just need to ask God in faith for forgiveness and His gift of eternal life. The following prayer is one you can use as a pattern.

> *Dear Lord Jesus, I know I am a sinner, and I ask for Your forgiveness. I believe You died for my sins and rose from the dead. I want to turn from my sins and trust in You as my Lord and Saviour. I invite You now to come into my heart and life. In Your Name. Amen.*

If you've just prayed this prayer from your heart and believe every word, you are now following Jesus. Well done! This will turn your life around in a wonderful way. You have no idea how happy you've just made the angels in heaven since the Bible tells us they celebrate and rejoice over each person who turns to God.

In fact, Jesus uses a parable of a shepherd to depict this celebration (Luke 15:1-7). The shepherd discovers that one of his hundred sheep is missing. So he leaves the other ninety-nine woolly creatures safely in a paddock and sets out into the night to look for the one that is lost.

When he finally finds the missing sheep, he hoists it on his shoulders. Why? Probably because the sheep was too cold and frightened to walk. Once the little creature is back with the rest of the flock, the shepherd gathers his friends and neighbours together to celebrate over the missing sheep's safe return.

To the average person who has never raised sheep, throwing a party over just one lost and found sheep might seem a little extreme. But Jesus goes on to make clear we are the sheep, and our loving Shepherd will go to any extreme, including His death on the cross, to bring us safely into the fold.

> *Rejoice with me; I have found my lost sheep. I tell you that in the same way there will be more rejoicing in heaven over one sinner who repents than over ninety-nine righteous persons who do not need to repent . . . In the same way, I tell you, there is rejoicing in the presence of the angels of God over one sinner who repents."*
> *(Luke 15:6-7, 10, NIV)*

The message in this story couldn't be clearer and almost leaps off the page. Jesus willingly gave His life on the cross to save lost sinners from eternal harm in hell because He loves us so much. And every individual person on this earth is as important as all the others in His eyes because we all matter to Him. He is not willing to lose even one member of His flock (2 Peter 3:9).

So if you harbour any concern in your heart that you are somehow too sinful, broken, or unworthy for Jesus to extend His forgiveness and redemption, believe me that you are not. If God could extend His loving mercy and grace to me, I promise He longs to do so to you as well. At the end of the day, we are all broken vessels. But the good news is that God is the potter and we are the clay.

> *But now, O LORD, You are our Father; We are the clay, and You our potter; And all we are the work of Your hand. (Isaiah 64:8, NKJV)*

In other words, God has the power to repair our brokenness and make us new again. How awesome is that?

27

Epilogue

Your life is like a book.
~ Grenville Kleiser

Well, dear reader, for the second time (assuming you've read my first book, *Hidden Thorns*), we've come to the end of our time together. Before we say our farewells, let me just express what a great honour it has been to share with you in these pages the messages God has laid on my heart for all who are willing to listen.

We each have a story worth telling. Just how our story turns out and what others will take away from it depends on our life choices, actions, attitudes, character, and service to God and others. I love the following quote from American inspirational author and speaker Grenville Kleiser.

Your life is like a book. The title page is your name. The preface is your introduction to the world. The pages are a daily chronicle of your efforts, trials, pleasures, discouragements, ambition, and achievements. Day by day your thoughts and acts are being inscribed as evidence of your success or failure. Hour by hour the record is being made which must stand for all time. One day the word "Finis" must be written. Let it then be said of your book that it is a record of purpose, generous service and work well done.

In that context, if our lives are like a book, another quote accredited to nineteenth century British writer William J. Thoms gives us a powerful reminder every follower of God should heed.

Be careful how you live. You may be the only Bible some people ever read.

I certainly pray that the "Bible" people are reading of my own life is bringing glory to my Saviour. After plodding uphill for many years, this season of my heart is a time of abundance for me. I'm traipsing thought lush meadows of warm sunshine, and I don't want it to end. Of course, the day will come as for all of us when the word "Finis" will be written, and I will also rejoice in stepping into the final season of the heart, eternal life in heaven. In the meantime, I chose to embrace God's gift of life with open arms. It's all about believing and receiving His blessing, but more importantly it's a time to rejoice and be glad.

I began writing my story with the goal of sharing several core messages God laid on my heart. With *Hidden Thorns*, where I bared my soul in telling the story of my daughter's loss, my focus was to walk you through to my own realisation through God's Spirit that I had to forgive my daughter's murderer. To do that, I needed first to seek my own forgiveness from God since the Bible tells us we are to forgive others as God forgives us (Matthew 6:14; 18:21-35; Ephesians 4:32).

In writing *Precious Whispers,* a passionate desire has been to fight against the evil that took my daughter's life, domestic violence. This is not a challenge anyone can effectively accomplish on their own. But we can do so as a body, which is why I've sought to raise awareness of the dangers to society with the aim of preventing another senseless murder. Even if I barely scratch the surface of this cause and one person's life is spared because of it, I will be happy knowing I gave it my all.

But the most significant purpose hands-down in writing this book is to share with you, my reader, my personal growth as a Christian through the "new normal" of this horrific event and its aftermath. Going through trials and tribulations ignited the need to depend on God's grace more and more each day. Just as flowers can sprout in the most desolate places, I've blossomed in a landscape of grief and pain into a stronger, more confident woman whose heart desire is to keep growing in faith, lovingly guided by my heavenly Father's precious whispers. I've learned to be grateful through hard times and difficult journeys, putting my trust in God regardless of circumstances.

I've also learned to sit back and be content with where God has placed me in life rather than frenetically striving for "bigger and better." I love the words of King David in Psalm 131, where he encourages us not to aim at high and mighty things but to be humbly content with who God has created us to be the way a toddler is content curled up on a mother's lap.

> *My heart is not proud, Lord, my eyes are not haughty; I do not concern myself with great matters or things too wonderful for me.But I have calmed and quieted myself, I am like a weaned child with its mother; like a weaned child I am content. (Psalm 131:1-2)*

These words speak volumes to my heart and soul, and I've claimed King David's own aspirations to be like a contented child on our loving heavenly Parent's lap as my own. In fact, when I look back at who I once was, a person I hardly recognise now, I ask myself in disbelief, "Is this really you, Marie-Rose? The same person whose heart was broken in a million pieces and could not be consoled? My, how you've grown!"

Indeed, I've come a long way and learned so much. I'll always be grateful for the lessons of the heart God has taught me along the journey. One that sticks out for me is the importance of applying prayer to every situation, not only for myself but for others as well. So please feel free to ask me to pray for you and any needs you may have. I would consider it a privilege to be a "God-appointed agent" to come before God's throne on your behalf. Incidentally, I stumbled across another quote recently I think you will agree is a definite takeaway.

> *God has no PHONE, but I talk to Him.*
> *God has no FACEBOOK, but He is still my friend.*
> *God has no TWITTER, but I still follow Him.*

Amen! So very true in my life and I pray in yours as well. And now it's with a bit of sadness that I come to the end of our time together. My sincere thanks to you, dear reader, for allowing me to share my own ongoing experience of God's precious whispers and seasons of the heart. My hope and prayer for each of you reading these pages is that you will find its contents helpful and applicable to your own journey through life.

And if you in turn would like to share with me some of your own heart story, ask me to pray for you, or even join with me in the cause of ending domestic violence in our nation, please visit my website at *https://marie-rosefox.au* and do drop me a note or follow me on Twitter. Praise You, Yahweh Shalom, the God of Peace, for peace is exactly what the world needs right now.

FINIS CORONAT OPUS
Ecclesiastes 7:8

Marie-Rose Fox was born in Portugal. She relocated with her family to France, where she spent most of her teenage years. While there, she developed a great love for languages, over time adding French, Spanish, Italian, and English to her Portuguese. At eighteen, she immigrated with her family to Australia. She resided in Sydney most of her adult life until moving to the Gold Coast of Queensland. Marie-Rose has enjoyed a multifaceted career experience in public service, business administration, sales, and beauty therapy before founding with husband Stephen their own company, Perfect Water Systems. Tragedy entered her life in 2007 when her only child Michelle was brutally murdered, a story told in Marie-Rose's first book title *Hidden Thorns* along with her personal journey of faith, healing, forgiveness, and God's love.